volume 50

CONCEPT MAPPING FOR PLANNING AND EVALUATION

APPLIED SOCIAL RESEARCH METHODS SERIES

Edited by Leonard Bickman and Debra J. Rog

APPLIED SOCIAL RESEARCH
METHODS SERIES

Series Editors

LEONARD BICKMAN, Peabody College, Vanderbilt University, Nashville
DEBRA J. ROG, Vanderbilt University, Washington, DC

volume 50

CONCEPT MAPPING FOR PLANNING AND EVALUATION

Mary Kane
William M. K. Trochim

APPLIED SOCIAL RESEARCH METHODS SERIES
Edited by Leonard Bickman and Debra J. Rog

SAGE Publications
Thousand Oaks ■ London ■ New Delhi

For information:

Sage Publications, Inc.
2455 Teller Road
Thousand Oaks, California 91320
E-mail: order@sagepub.com

Sage Publications Ltd.
1 Oliver's Yard
55 City Road
London EC1Y 1SP
United Kingdom

Sage Publications India Pvt. Ltd.
B–42, Panchsheel Enclave
Post Box 4109
New Delhi 110 017 India

Printed in the United States of America

Library of Congress Cataloging-in-Publication Data

Kane, Mary.
Concept mapping for planning and evaluation / Mary Kane and William M. K. Trochim.
    p. cm.—(Applied social research methods series; 50)
Includes bibliographical references and index.
ISBN 1-4129-4027-3 or 978-1-4129-4027-6 (cloth)
ISBN 1-4129-4028-1 or 978-1-4129-4028-3 (pbk.)
    1. Social sciences—Methodology. 2. Information visualization.
  I. Trochim, William M. K. II. Title.
H61.T724 2007
300.1'154—dc22

                                                    2006017537

This book is printed on acid-free paper.

06   07   08   09   10   10   9   8   7   6   5   4   3   2   1

Acquisitions Editor:	Lisa Cuevas Shaw
Associate Editor:	Margo Beth Crouppen
Editorial Assistant:	Karen Margrethe Greene
Production Editor:	Melanie Birdsall
Copy Editor:	Barbara Ray
Typesetter:	C&M Digitals (P) Ltd.
Indexer:	Sheila Bodell
Cover Designer:	Candice Harman

Contents

Preface

Human beings derive meaning from being part of a group. The way we live, communicate, and plan for the future is based on our interactions with groups, and particularly our efforts to understand and build consensus within them. Since the development of the systematic study of groups, social scientists have attempted to develop rigorous, participatory approaches for groups to harness these efforts to plan better, act effectively, and then assess or evaluate their efforts.

An equally human activity is the making of maps—to help us know where we are, our choices for moving from here to some new place, and how to go home again. World globes, road maps, or water markings all link us to the territory upon which we stand and the directions we go in when we change. The concept mapping methodology presented in this book is part of a lengthy evolution in how we map a topology of thought and knowledge and put it to use for the benefit of the human activities of planning and measuring changes.

Planning and evaluation are essential human activities, aided by the intelligence, knowledge, and experience that individuals bring to the creation of a common approach to any issue. Planning and evaluation both involve many people and positions, and individuals often approach the tasks with their own knowledge, experiences, and political perspectives. Recognizing the value and range of individuals' perspectives in the creation of a common framework is one of the biggest methodological challenges that planners and evaluators face.

Concept mapping takes into account both the human characteristics of social group connections and the desire to identify the terrain, using both a quantitative and qualitative approach to an area where words, voices, and even data can often fail us. The most vocal participants, the most common statements, or the most forcefully expressed ideas may represent the core views of a diverse stakeholder group—or they may not. Concept mapping is a methodology that creates a stakeholder-authored visual geography of ideas from many communities of interest, combined with specific analysis and data interpretation methods, to produce maps that can then be used to guide planning and evaluation efforts on the issues that matter to the group.

Other techniques have been proposed in the past for the mapping of ideas. Novak (1984) describes a "free-hand" concept mapping procedure that involves the articulation of major ideas and classification of them into hierarchical concepts. Rico (1983) has advocated "free-hand" concept mapping or drawing as a useful method for developing a conceptual framework for writing. Moore (1987) describes the use of several strategies for developing ideas—the nominal group technique, idea writing, Delphi technique, and interpretive structural modeling—all of which could result in maps or pictures. These and other approaches have value for planning and evaluation, but fall outside of the scope of this volume.

The concept mapping method described here differs from other concept mapping techniques for several reasons:

- It is purposefully designed to integrate input from multiple sources with differing content expertise or interest.

- It creates a series of maps that depict the composite thinking of the group.

- It uses multivariate data analyses to construct the maps.

- It generates interval-level maps that have unique advantages for planning and evaluation, especially through pattern matching and go-zone analysis (described later in this volume).

- Its resulting data are well suited to bivariate comparisons across variables such as rating criteria, stakeholder groups, different points in time, or other criteria, to aid in targeted planning, implementation strategies, and evaluation.

The process discussed throughout this volume is one of a range of existing structured conceptualization processes. Group concept mapping is related to the growing interest in the role that theory plays in planning and evaluation. In evaluation, for instance, this interest is seen in writings on the importance of program theory (Bickman, 1986; Chen & Rossi, 1983, 1987); in the increased emphasis on the importance of studying causal process (Mark, 1986); in the recognition of the central role of judgment—especially theory-based judgment—in research (Cordray, 1986; Einhorn & Hogarth, 1986); and in the thinking of critical multiplism (Shadish, Cook, & Houts, 1986), which emphasizes the role of theory in selecting and guiding the analysis of multiple operationalizations. Concept mapping is one way to articulate theory in these contexts.

In planning, conceptualization has received somewhat more attention and is seen in the sometimes daunting proliferation of different planning models and methods of conceptualizing (Dunn, 1981; Moore, 1987). As tools for evaluation, such methods have found growing utility within projects whose outcomes represent a broad range of stakeholder objectives, particularly in cases where these objectives may evolve over time. In both contexts, concept mapping encompasses a participatory approach that has become increasingly valued and useful within a world of systems thinking and growing networks of organizations.

Since its introduction almost 20 years ago, the concept mapping methodology we describe in this volume has played a key role in a wide range of planning and evaluation projects; the following is a small sample:

- Allocation of tobacco settlement funds in Hawaii, deriving recommendations that were subsequently implemented by the Hawaii state legislature (Trochim, Milstein, Wood, Jackson, & Pressler, 2004)

- Examining barriers to African American families' involvement in the treatment of their family members with mental illness (Biegel, Johnsen, & Shafran, 1997)

- Exploring gender differences in perceptions of sexual harassment in the workplace (Hurt, Wiener, Russell, & Mannen, 1999)

- Developing a business design training program for a management consulting firm, identifying training needs and related expected competencies for facilitator/consultants in business organizations, and assessing staff capacity (McLinden & Trochim, 1998; McLinden & Trochim, 1998)

- Defining priorities for end-of-life issues within the public health community, across stakeholders including public health officials, professionals in advocacy, academic and policy positions, members of a prevention research network, and others (Rao et al., 2005)

- Developing a model of the needs of children in pediatric hospice and palliative care (Donnelly, Huff, Lindsey, McMahon, & Schumacher, 2005)

- Establishing guidelines for the public health management of lower-prevalence chronic conditions such as epilepsy, under the guidance of the Centers for Disease Control and Chronic Disease Directors (Wheeler et al., 2005)

- Identifying conceptual domains that providers of complementary and alternative medicine would emphasize in survey studies (Baldwin, Kroesen, Trochim, & Bell, 2004)

- Developing a model of the problems of persons with traumatic brain injury (Donnelly, Donnelly, & Grohman, 2005)

This volume is an authoritative guide to the methodology and strategies behind using concept mapping for a broad range of social scientists, including students, researchers, and practitioners. It gives special attention to the issues facing the facilitator of a concept mapping project, where the authors share considerable real-world experience in planning and implementing these projects, together with extensive content on the technical underpinnings of this method and its key issues in analysis and results interpretation. Finally, closing chapters on using concept mapping in planning and evaluation show some of the many ways concept mapping can be applied in practice, together with detailed examples from actual practice.

The philosopher William James once stated that, "Ideas are so much flat psychological surface, unless some mirrored matter gives them cognitive lustre." Concept mapping represents a unique method for mirroring the ideas of a group, in a way that creates insight, understanding, and consensus. This volume will help you see beyond the flat topography to uncover the geography of ideas that has remained unseen and leverage these ideas to the benefit of your own social science efforts.

Acknowledgments

One day, some time over the last three or four years, we quietly and unceremoniously passed the 20th anniversary of the concept mapping methodology that is the focus of this volume. As with most things in our lives, we can't know the exact date of its inception, and it probably doesn't even make sense to think of discrete beginnings in this case. The methodology has deep foundations, certainly back to the middle of the last century, and its traditions and underlying theory reach back much further than that. But the evolutionary pathway that led to this volume does have discernable markings, and many people played critically important roles along the way. We hope to acknowledge several here, and ask forgiveness of those whom we do not mention or have inadvertently neglected.

The track we are on certainly traces to the founding work of Bill Trochim in the early 1980s. An unremarkable conversation with a graduate student, Dorothy Torre, about the baffling construct of empowerment led Bill to suggest, in some degree of frustration, that she spend a week brainstorming as many ideas related to that construct as she could. The next week, when she dutifully returned with the list in hand, Bill's next thought was a natural and undistinguished one—to categorize or group the ideas by theme. That proved decidedly unsatisfying—there were clearly multiple ways to group so complex a set of issues. So they did several sorts, only to face the challenge of what to do with that information. This was not so easily resolved, and it led to something a bit more unpredictable: the insight that we could aggregate different unstructured sorts of the same set of items into a single similarity matrix. Although he did not realize it at the time, Trochim had independently reinvented this method of sorting aggregation. What, then, should be done with the aggregated matrix? The first impulse would have been some form of factor analysis. But when he was a graduate student at Northwestern University in the late 1970s, Trochim had taken a graduate class with then post-doc Will Shadish, who had spent perhaps one class session introducing the more obscure methodology of multidimensional scaling. Some investigating confirmed that the method would be appropriate for sort similarity matrices and the concept mapping methodology, although cluster analysis also had promise. So, both were applied to the matrix and concept mapping had its core technology and its characterizing integration of qualitative and quantitative, of mathematical and visual.

Shortly thereafter, a large multiunit department at Cornell, the Division of Campus Life, asked Professor Trochim if he would assist them in a major strategic planning effort. He agreed, but only if they would use the new methodology he was in the process of constructing as an integral part. This commenced a long succession of local projects that engaged Trochim and a dynamic group of graduate students. Foremost among these was Rhoda Linton, who brought to the method her keen sensitivity to process and knowledge of feminist research methodology (Linton, 1989b). Rhoda played a critical role in the formulation of the methodology as it was implemented then, completing the first doctoral dissertation that used it and co-authoring with Trochim (Trochim & Linton, 1986) one of the first two publications about the method that offered a general taxonomy of conceptualization methods that can still be distinguished in the core steps of the process today. The graduate students who took part in these early years are too numerous to list entirely, but included Kathy Valentine (1989), James Davis (1989), Jules Marquart (1989), Val Caracelli (1989b), Pat Galvin (1989), Leslie Cooksy (1989), Mark Mannes (1989), Doug Keith (1989), and Jeanne Dumont (1989), each of whom contributed articles to the 1989 special issue of *Evaluation and Program Planning* devoted to the concept mapping methodology (Trochim, 1989a). Thus began a long tradition of graduate research use of the method that has led to over 60 dissertations and theses. In this path we wish to acknowledge directly the outstanding contributions of Sarita Davis, Dominic Cirillo, Edie (Lassegard) Cook, Saumitra Sengupta, Deb Hover, Nicole Driebe, Matt Davidson, Don Weir, David Diehl, Darl Kolb, Jeff Wellstead, Jon Gans, and both Naomi Penney and Naomi Penney Degan (mother and daughter). As this graduate student community expanded outside of Cornell, it came to include Tom Grayson (University of Illinois), Gerry Florio (University of Buffalo), Greg Michalski (University of Ottawa), and Eric Nelson (University of Illinois). This proud tradition continues with current graduate students working in this method, including Jen Brown, Anna Waldron, and David Filiberto. Derek Cabrera currently plays a key role in helping to lead the concept mapping method into the newest frontiers of systems thinking and the complexity sciences.

Faculty colleagues and notable mentors of graduate students who have used the concept mapping method include Jim Donnelly (University of Buffalo), Brad Cousins (University of Ottawa), and Peter Calder (University of Alberta). Nick Smith (Syracuse University) generously reviewed the earliest drafts of this manuscript. Mike Duttweiler has been both a major user and supporter of concept mapping, from his work helping to produce the only video documentary on the method to his current efforts to support its use in the Cooperative Extension system. We wish especially to recognize the roles that Don Tobias played throughout the evolution of concept mapping, as champion and proponent, and co-facilitator in too many projects to list, from the Buddhist monastery in Yonkers to aging issues in the state of Texas. Among the research collaborators we have had the pleasure to work with, we would like to acknowledge Belle Ruth Witkin, Bobby Milstein, and Tom Chapel. Friends and colleagues who became partners in using and expanding the Concept Systems approach include Ken Oakley, Tina Rosenblum, and Diane Gayeski.

Along with the development of this academic and research community, the software evolution that began in the mid-1980s with the original software program in BASIC on an Apple II computer, subsequently migrated to the Microsoft MS-DOS platform, then to Windows and the Web today. At the same time, the Concept Systems company was founded, first as an unincorporated and informal business venture (Naomi Penney the First was the first purchaser of the software in 1987—and bought two copies!).

Many others played key roles in the software evolution story. Early on, a group at the Education and Training Center at Anderson Worldwide included Larry Silvey, Dan McLinden, Bill Patterson, Darryl Jenkins, and Oliver Cummings, and subsequently drew in Cornell graduates Rose (Jusko) Setze and Matt Tobias. Early corporate client work led us to like-minded souls like George Doherty and son Joel, Tony Gifford, Lee Mazanec, Jim Frazier at Motorola, and Neal Koenig at CITGO.

After several years of conducting community-based concept mapping as a "sideline," Mary Kane jumped into the development of Concept Systems in 1992 as its founding CEO and the guiding force ever since. Mary took the fundamental software and traditional focus group methodology surrounding it and developed integrated, comprehensive process methodologies to enable greater flexibility and reach for the process and its technology. Concept Systems Inc., incorporated in 1994, has been the proving ground for the expanded methodology and the development and testing team for software and technology innovations. An incredibly talented team of CSI employees and friends has aided this work, and continues to amaze and delight with their intelligence, innovative spirit, and client-centered focus, as well as their technical savvy. Very early on, Dan McLinden was a strong contributor, and since then the team has included bright lights like Heather Freeborn, Amy Hogan, Katy Hall, Brenda Pepe, and Melissa Burns. Lucy Staley focused CSI's operations, and Jodi Denman makes sure that CSI runs as a successful small business. Uniquely talented contributors—dedicated, thoughtful, multilevel thinkers—are Kathleen Quinlan and Jeanine Draut, who provide depth and breadth, innovation and sensitive process to our client relationships; and Chris Grant and Matt Clark, the dynamic programming team who have guided CSI to the development of new technologies and programs in the CSGlobal and new analysis software.

Much of our research development and consulting experience with concept mapping has been concentrated in public health (Trochim & Kane, 2005) and medical research at the National Institutes of Health and the Centers for Disease Control and Prevention. The earliest funded research was the foundational grant from the National Institutes of Mental Health that began a continuing partnership and friendship with David Shern and initiated a tradition of concept mapping in mental health (Johnsen, Biegel, & Shafran, 2000; Trochim & Cook, 1992). Deciding to frame the TRIO (Turning Research Into Outcomes) initiative in NCI on the basis of concept mapping was Jon Kerner, whose belief in the value of concept mapping to enable a national comprehensive cancer plan to take hold fundamentally established Concept Systems' value to public health. Cynthia Vinson guided and supported over a dozen concept mapping initiatives under Jon's leadership. Jon introduced us to Lori Belle Isle at the ACS and Leslie Given at the CDC, who were willing co-conspirators in the early adoption of the Concept System approach for large scale public health framework development—the basis of much of our current work. Other NCI colleagues who continued to challenge and energize the methodology applications were Steve Marcus, Louise Masse, and Rick Moser. The staff of the Office on Behavioral and Social Science Research at the NIH, led by David Abrams, have become colleagues and co-designers in applications for planning using this approach.

CSI's work with the CDC has produced the kinds of colleague relationships that one wishes for with clients. Research and initiative clients who have become much more than that include Linda Anderson, Michael Dalmat, Jaya Rao, Suzanne Smith, Darwin Labarthe, and Abu Abdel Quadar. Sue Lin Yee was one of the first evaluators within the CDC to apply the CS approach to internal CDC needs. Janet Collins and Jim Marks were the NCCDPHP leaders who supported most of these new initiatives. Partners in innovation with the CDC were the National Association of Chronic Disease Directors and their committed teams of consultants and staff—like Fran Wheeler, who partners, challenges, and supports, always with a perfect South Carolina bon mot; and our friends Dennis Shepard, Sandy Adams, and Jeanne Alongi.

This book has had an incredible history. It has literally been nearly 20 years in the making, and came very close to never being born. Our deepest thanks to Len Bickman and Debra Rog for staying with us on this effort for most of their adult lives. And, for his responsive writing and editorial skills, we acknowledge Rich Gallagher, whose experience in these matters helped keep us on an even keel.

To those of you we've missed, know that you're a part of this effort. And to the many, many students, community groups, independent researchers, faculty researchers, advocates, and organizational staff who have used this methodology over the last 20 years: we acknowledge your own unique commitment to helping your organization get it right by enabling voices to be heard, ideas to be recognized and valued, and solutions to emerge. Thank you for your dedication.

It is common practice to dedicate a volume to one's spouse, because it is usually that person who should receive not only a dedication but often co-authorship as well. We took care of that problem by marrying each other 34 years ago; so, with the full understanding that we do and will continually dedicate our professional and personal endeavors to each other, we dedicate this joint effort to our most wonderful and most rewarding family endeavor, our daughter Nora.

1

An Introduction to Concept Mapping

Ideas are like rabbits. You get a couple and learn how to handle them, and pretty soon you have a dozen.

—John Steinbeck

Concept mapping is a generic term that describes any process for representing ideas in pictures or maps. In this book, however, we use the term only to refer to one specific form of concept mapping, an integrated approach (Trochim, 1989c; Trochim & Linton, 1986) whose steps include brainstorming, statement analysis and synthesis, unstructured sorting of statements, multidimensional scaling and cluster analysis, and the generation of numerous interpretable maps and data displays.

Concept mapping can be considered a structured methodology for organizing the ideas of a group or organization, to bring together diverse groups of stakeholders and help them rapidly form a common framework that can be used for planning, evaluation, or both. It can be considered a type of integrated mixed method (Caracelli & Greene, 1993; Greene, Caracelli, & Graham, 1989) because its qualitative and quantitative components are inextricably interwoven to enable a diverse group of stakeholders to articulate their ideas and represent them in a variety of quantitatively derived visual results—concept maps, pattern matches, and value plots—that can be used in reaching both awareness of the issues at hand and agreement on how to proceed.

This collaborative group process generates a conceptual framework for planning and evaluation that has several benefits for social scientists and other researchers, compared with less sophisticated conceptualization approaches such as focus groups:

- It represents a systematic process that integrates structured group processes such as brainstorming, unstructured idea sorting, and rating tasks with sophisticated multivariate statistical methods to produce a well-defined, quantitative set of results.
- It graphically represents a domain of ideas in a framework that can be utilized directly for developing specific planning objectives or evaluation metrics.
- It facilitates the collection of input from a broad and diverse array of stakeholder groups and/or other data sources, in virtually any setting in which a group issue

1

or need requires definition, planning, and evaluation, and it enables feedback on these data to participants in a timely manner.

- It can be used with stakeholder groups of any size, ranging from small single-site meetings to hundreds of geographically diverse stakeholders providing information on-line.

- It provides a collaborative, participatory process, involving stakeholders in communities of interest directly in the interpretation of the results as well as initial idea generation. The stakeholders themselves, rather than the facilitator, drive the content for the entire conceptualization and results interpretation process.

Above all, concept mapping employs a methodology that integrates the planning and evaluation process, providing a unified framework for both within a systems perspective (Veney & Kaluzny, 1984). By representing the efforts of participants as a geography of thought, across multiple communities of interest, it provides a new, quantitative framework for effective planning and evaluation efforts.

Concept mapping seeks the open contribution of participant stakeholders' ideas on a specific issue, organizes the ideas, and portrays them in pictures or maps that are readily understood. Using the resulting concept map as a foundation, researchers can measure any number of variables of interest—such as the importance or feasibility of participant ideas—and display them as patterns on the map. They can then compare two or more patterns—in the aggregate and in their details—using pattern matching to look at consensus and consistency over time, along with bivariate displays known as "go zones," to identify the potential courses of action or types of measurement. The concept mapping process is useful as an integrating framework throughout the life cycle of a project, from the initial conceptualization of the project, to the development of actions, programs, and/or measures, to the initial implementation of them, and finally to evaluation and reformulation.

Some examples in which concept mapping has been employed successfully include the following:

- The Hawaii Department of Health (HDOH) used concept mapping techniques to engage local stakeholders and national subject area experts to define the community and system factors that affect individuals' behaviors related to tobacco, nutrition, and physical activity (Trochim et al., 2004). The results were immediately incorporated into an official plan, approved by the governor and state legislature, that recommended how Hawaii's tobacco settlement resources could be used to create sustainable changes in population health. This project was completed within a four-week deadline and successfully resulted in DOH funding from Hawaii's share of this tobacco settlement. Moreover, the results provided a framework that will be employed for future program evaluation.

- Concept mapping was employed by a project sponsored by the National Association of Chronic Disease Directors (NACDD), in conjunction with the Centers for Disease Control and Prevention (CDC), to address the role that state health departments could play in addressing epilepsy and other low-prevalence chronic conditions (LPCCs) in the event that increased federal funding were to be made available. Stakeholders included representation from the CDD, the CDC, public health agencies, advocacy groups, and others. This project recommended a range of activities through which state health departments could become more involved with addressing epilepsy or other LPCCs, including assessment, epidemiology, and surveillance; partnerships; state plans; intervention; and evaluation. Moreover, these recommendations were remarkably consistent with previously established best-practices program components for state-based chronic disease programs.

- The National Cancer Institute (NCI) employed concept mapping as part of the evaluation of a large, complex center grant program known as the Transdisciplinary Tobacco User Research Centers (TTURCs) (Stokols et al., 2003). The mapping was done to help determine the outcomes to be measured as a basis for evaluation. In this project, the use of concept maps clarified not only clusters of ideas, but a regionalization of these clusters into areas defining the process, structure, and outcomes of their efforts—leading to an almost exact mapping of these cluster groups into short-term, intermediate, and long-term evaluation criteria, as discussed in Chapter 8.

A researcher can implement concept mapping over the life course of a planning or evaluation project to help address many of the fundamental design, process, and outcome questions that are inherent to these projects:

- *What are the issues in a planning or evaluation project?* Concept mapping commences with development of specific focus and rating prompts, which require articulation of specific issues and desired outcomes, followed by a structured brainstorming process to generate stakeholder ideas. Moreover, the natural applicability of this process to the World Wide Web facilitates gathering ideas from large and geographically dispersed communities of interest.

- *Which issues are relatively more important or should have higher priority?* A sorting and rating process, driven by the stakeholders, provides raw data for a sophisticated, mixed-method analysis of how ideas are clustered and rated by participants.

- *Is there consensus among participant groups?* Concept mapping analysis produces visual displays of how the ratings of individual stakeholder subgroups agree or diverge.

- *Do the stakeholders have a common vision of what they are trying to achieve that enables them to stay on track throughout the life cycle of a project?* The visual maps clarify core ideas for the participants—how they are clustered, how they relate to each other, and how they are rated along specified criteria. Groups use this information to recognize the "current state" of their thinking and to track changes.

- *Are stakeholders able to assess the implementation of programs or interventions and check on the degree to which they reflect the originally intended focus, bridging the gap between planning and evaluation?* The concept mapping methodology provides a common framework for assessing both planning efforts and subsequent program evaluation.

- *Does the program work, and on which variables is it working?* The concept mapping approach of operating on both specific ideas and clusters of ideas and their associated rating values, enables the evaluation of specific aspects of program results. It also facilitates program evaluation across both time and the perspectives of multiple stakeholder groups.

- *Can stakeholders link program outcomes to original expectations or intentions to see if they are achieving what they set out to achieve?* By employing a concept mapping methodology, program evaluators can generate relevant outcome criteria as a natural output of the planning process.

- *What does our organization's evaluation system consist of, and how it is implemented?* Concept mapping develops a system framework and enables an organization to connect its requirements, progress indicators, and measures in an integrated way.

Concept mapping addresses questions like these within planning and evaluation projects by combining quantitative and qualitative analysis methods with participatory group processes, in a way that clarifies the understanding and analysis of overall stakeholder thought. It helps individuals to think more effectively as a group, but without losing the uniqueness of their individual contributions. It also helps the groups to manage the inherent complexity in most planning and evaluation situations without trivializing or losing important detail.

The conceptualization of an issue becomes the key to tangible outcomes in planning and evaluation. To develop a model like the ones above assumes that researchers understand the issue that the plan is supposed to address, fix, or improve. To conduct evaluation assumes that they can identify and measure the elements that will reflect the need and also show desired change. Conceptualizing the issue and drawing from that conceptualization a relevant approach to planning and evaluation are critical steps that are often challenging for applied researchers.

Social research uses many ways to accomplish the conceptualization task, but this volume is not an attempt to review all existing methods. Instead, we describe a specific process—concept mapping—that has been investigated in some detail over the course of the last two decades and is recognized as a valuable tool in planning and evaluation. It makes outcomes like the ones described above possible through a process of brainstorming, statement synthesis, analysis, and mapping, which support conceptualization of issues by researchers. This chapter introduces concept mapping and shows how it works throughout the life cycle of a project. The chapters that follow describe each of the steps necessary to complete an appropriate and successful concept mapping project.

PLANNING AND EVALUATION
IN THE PROJECT LIFE CYCLE

At the most general level, planning and evaluation tend to follow a rather simple process over the life of a project, as outlined in Figure 1.1.

In the first phase, *conceptualization,* the key stakeholders identify the major issues, try to make sense of them, and usually try to achieve some consensus or shared vision regarding what is to be done. If they are developing a program, they might try to come to agreement about the program's goals and objectives and delineate the important components or elements of the program.

In the second phase, *development,* some stakeholders begin to translate the conceptual framework into operational reality. They describe each phase of program delivery, the resources that are needed, and exactly how the work might best be accomplished.

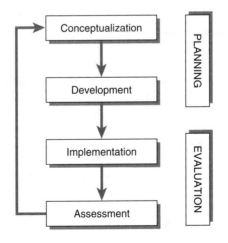

Figure 1.1 A Typical Project Life Cycle

In phase three, *implementation,* the program or plan is pilot-tested and the fidelity to the original vision is checked. If needed, the program is fine-tuned and adjusted to reflect more accurately what was intended.

Finally, in the fourth phase, *assessment,* the effects of the program are evaluated, both on short-term measures and on longer-term indicators of success or performance. The evaluation often leads to the initiation of an entirely new cycle with a more informed reconceptualization of the problem and a new, perhaps changed shared vision.

This project life cycle model highlights the general stages in almost any project. The detailed procedures would certainly differ depending on the nature of the project. For instance, the development phase methodology for designing a social program would be very different from the process for designing an interactive multimedia training program. Nevertheless, at this highest level, most projects follow some variation of the stages described in the figure.

Although planners and evaluators have described numerous variations of the project life cycle (Veney & Kaluzny, 1984), they usually lack a methodology for integrating all of its stages. A complex, multiphase structure like the one described above makes it a challenge to maintain a continuity of effort over the entire life cycle in the absence of an integrated methodology such as concept mapping. Multiple stakeholder groups are involved at different phases of most projects, each bringing their own values, perspectives, and preferences to the project. Unless there are methods that enable such multiphase projects to remain on track, miscommunication and disconnection can easily occur among groups and between stages.

The concept mapping model is a comprehensive approach that addresses the entire project life cycle. Suppose that you are a social researcher examining how to disseminate evidence-based health care practices effectively and then measure the effectiveness of these dissemination strategies. Using concept mapping at the very beginning of a project such as this helps the various stakeholder groups lay out their ideas for the project, organize these ideas, and explore consensus. It helps structure the shared vision in the form of a concept map that can guide detailed project development efforts. It can provide the framework to assess the initial implementation of the program and help assure that it is faithful to the program vision. It also enables evaluators to track the outcomes from the program, both immediate and longer term, to assess the degree to which the program is achieving what was intended and to suggest ways that the program could be continually improved.

For most applications, particularly in the social sciences, both planning and evaluation activities involve the articulation of thoughts, ideas, or hunches, and the representation of these in some objective form. Although some view planning and evaluation as distinct activities, we believe that they are necessary phases of one process and ought to be interlinked. This methodology approaches both from a common systems perspective—as the analysis and interpretation of a geography of ideas. Foundationally, concept mapping as described here applies integrative mixed methods and connects structured group processes with several sophisticated multivariate statistical methods.

The Concept Mapping Process

In the concept mapping method, groups of ideas are represented in the form of a picture or map—creating a visual, geographic representation of the topic of interest. To construct the map, the ideas are first described or generated and the interrelationships between them are articulated. Multivariate statistical techniques—multidimensional scaling and cluster analysis—are then applied to this information and the results depicted in map form. The content of the map (the group of ideas) is entirely determined by the participant group. The group brainstorms the initial ideas, provides information about how these ideas are related, interprets the results of the analyses, and decides how the map is to be used.

This concept mapping approach is effective when a group of people wants to develop a conceptual framework for evaluation or planning. The framework, which may describe the current state of an issue or a future desired state, is displayed as a series of concept maps that graphically represent the group's thinking. These maps display all of the group's ideas relative to the topic at hand, showing how these ideas are related to each other and, usually, showing which ideas are more relevant, important, or appropriate.

Concept mapping is particularly effective when known groups of multiple stakeholders, such as multiagency steering committees, are involved in planning and evaluation efforts. Groups like these might consist of the administrators, staff, or members of the board of directors of an organization; community leaders or representatives of relevant constituency groups; academicians or members of the policymaking community; funding agents or representatives of groups with oversight responsibility; groups of researchers and practitioners in specific areas of inquiry; representatives of relevant client populations; or combinations of these. Less appropriate to concept mapping as a tool are systems or cultures in which a hierarchical decision model is the norm or in which an organization's planning or evaluation models are predetermined.

The concept mapping process is guided by a *facilitator*, who could be an outside consultant or an internal member of the group responsible for the planning or evaluation effort. The facilitator manages the process, but the content, interpretation, and utilization of the concept map are determined entirely by the group. This facilitation process may be performed by a single person or a team and may involve people from inside or outside the organization.

Figure 1.2 shows an overview of the concept mapping process.

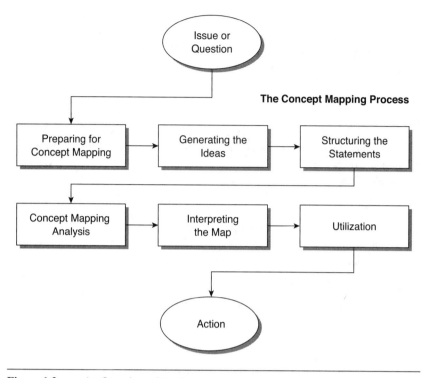

Figure 1.2   An Overview of the Concept Mapping Process

Table 1.1 describes the critical elements of each of the steps.

The details behind these steps form the basis of a design for implementing a concept mapping project. Here, we briefly describe the steps, and show an example that illustrates each step as it is applied in a hypothetical example of the entire process. Each step is the subject of a subsequent chapter in this volume.

Step 1: Preparing for Concept Mapping

The facilitator helps to manage the beginning of the process, working with a group of key participants to set the structure, expectations, and desired outcomes. To begin, the facilitator works with the client or sponsor to ensure that desired outcomes of the effort are clearly articulated. The facilitator then helps

Table 1.1
Steps in a Concept Mapping Process

1. Preparing for Concept Mapping
    *   *Focus.* The desired outcome of a study
    *   *Sampling and Participants.* Identifying relevant stakeholders and how they will be engaged
    *   *Scheduling and Logistics.* Orchestrating stakeholder participation

2. Generating the Ideas
    *   *Brainstorming.* Gathering knowledge and opinions
    *   *Ideas Analysis.* Creating a rationalized set of group ideas

3. Structuring the Statements
    *   *Demographics (Organization and/or Personal).* Identifying stakeholder groups for comparative analysis
    *   *Unstructured Pile Sorting.* Organizing ideas into groups
    *   *Rating(s).* Assigning values to ideas

4. Concept Mapping Analysis
    *   *Multidimensional Scaling*
    *   *Hierarchical Cluster Analysis*
    *   *Bridging Analysis*
    *   *Production of Maps*
    *   *Pattern Matching*
    *   *Bivariate Plots ("Go Zone" Plots)*

5. Interpreting the Maps
    *   *Structured, Participatory, Stakeholder-Based Interpretation.* Developing joint stakeholder authorship

6. Utilization
    *   *Action.* Action items from a planning process
    *   *Measurement.* Comparison of results against initial desired outcomes
    *   *Evaluation.* Connecting measures to the desired outcomes and assessing change

the group arrive at a specific focus for the project and helps ensure the selection of relevant participant stakeholders.

Developing the Focus. The first important step in preparation is developing the focus or domain of the conceptualization. Two separate focus statements are usually used to provide the direction for concept mapping. First, the facilitator guides participants in defining the focus for the brainstorming session, which is Step 2 of the process. Second, the participants and facilitator develop the focus for ratings that are performed during Step 3, the structuring step of the process. This focus defines the dimension(s) on which each of the brainstormed statements will be rated.

The focus for brainstorming is often first expressed as a *focus statement*, which is worded to give the specific instruction intended. For example, the brainstorming focus statement in a strategic planning process might be worded as follows:

"Generate short phrases or sentences that describe specific things that Organization XYZ should do to address its mission."

To facilitate the brainstorming process, this focus statement is then often recast as a *focus prompt*, worded in a complete-the-sentence format:

"One specific thing Organization XYZ needs to do in order to address its mission is . . ."

The focus prompt is typically arrived at through facilitated inquiry as to the desired outcomes and requirements of the initiative.

An *importance* rating focus for a program evaluation might be worded like this:

"Rate each potential outcome on a five point scale in terms of its importance to the program, where '1' means 'Not at all important,' '3' means 'Moderately important,' and '5' means 'Extremely important.'"

Ratings can be collected on any measure of interest to the project at hand, like priority, current capability, relevance to mission, preference, and so on. The group should agree on the specific wording for each of these rating scale statements.

Selecting the Participants. Identifying the participants in a concept mapping process is one of the most important tasks. Concept mapping is most useful when it includes a range of people whose knowledge or experience is relevant to the question, although some situations (e.g., product development planning) call for smaller, more homogeneous groups because the map's use is very targeted and other logistics are easier to accommodate. There is no strict limit on the number of participants; concept mapping projects have ranged from small groups of 8 to 15 people to ones involving hundreds of participants. In the early days of the method, participant groups tended to involve a relatively small group meeting in a single location; now, interactive tools employing the World Wide Web enable larger groups of participants spread across remote geographic locations to participate in brainstorming, sorting, and rating at their convenience.

It is not necessary that all participants take part in every step of the process. For instance, a large group may complete the generation (i.e., brainstorming) step; a much smaller group may perform the sorting task; and the same large group that generated the content may be responsible for rating the ideas. This model is particularly useful in projects with large groups of stakeholders. In general, however, we have found that concept maps are better understood by people who have participated in all phases of the process than by those who have taken part in only one or two steps.

Step 2: Generating the Ideas

Once the participants and focus statements have been defined, the actual concept mapping process begins. The participants generate a set of statements that, ideally, will represent the entire conceptual domain for the topic of interest. In a typical case, brainstorming is used and the focus prompt constitutes the basis for the brainstorming process. The usual rules for brainstorming apply (Osborn, 1948). People are encouraged to generate many statements and are told that there should be no criticism or discussion regarding the legitimacy of statements that are generated during the process. This process may take place in the form of a live meeting, where a facilitator records the statements as they are generated so that all members of the group can see the set of statements as they evolve; or occur remotely and asynchronously via the Internet or other means.

Ideas Analysis. Theoretically, there is no limit to the number of statements that can be processed, but large numbers of statements impose serious practical constraints in the subsequent participant activities. Because it is not unusual nowadays for hundreds of statements to be brainstormed, particularly in large, distributed groups of stakeholders, we often subsequently employ a process for analyzing and editing the statements to a more manageable set. This process always involves members of the stakeholder group. On the basis of our experience, we typically limit the final set of statements to 100 or fewer. This enables breadth of representation of contributed ideas while providing sorting and rating participants with manageable tasks to complete, as described below.

Step 3: Structuring the Statements

Once the group has a set of statements describing the conceptual domain for a given focus, we usually ask each participant to perform two "structuring" tasks—grouping (or sorting) and rating. For the grouping or sorting task (Coxon, 1999; Rosenberg & Kim, 1975; Weller & Romney, 1988), each person is instructed to group the ideas into piles "in a way that makes sense to you." Participants may not sort all items into *one* pile, sort every statement as its own pile (although *some* items may be grouped by themselves), or sort an item into more than one pile.

Participants can perform this sorting process either manually or electronically. The manual method involves printing each statement on a separate card and having each participant physically sort the cards into piles. This method has the advantage that you can spread all of the card piles in front of you and see them all simultaneously. Alternatively, a Web-based interface enables participants to sort by selecting statements from a list and clicking on a button to move them into the appropriate group. The Web-based method is the electronic equivalent of the manual process.

For the rating, each participant rates each statement on one or more dimensions as described in the rating focus statement. For example, the following is a *feasibility* rating focus prompt:

> "Rate each issue on a five point scale in terms of the feasibility of accomplishing it within the next three years, where '1' means 'Not at all feasible,' '3' means 'Moderately feasible,' and '5' means 'Extremely feasible.'"

Although many researchers apply a Likert-type response scale, any numeric scale can be used to elicit judgments from the participants. Here, as well, participants can either perform this step manually via pencil and paper or electronically with a software tool. In the analysis, the arithmetic mean of the ratings (and sometimes other descriptive statistical information) will be computed.

Step 4: Concept Mapping Analysis

The concept maps are computed at this stage with a multidimensional scaling analysis, which locates each statement as a separate point on a map. Statements that are closer to each other on this map are generally grouped together by the sorters more frequently; more distant statements on the map are in general grouped together less frequently. Next, a hierarchical cluster analysis partitions the statements on this map into clusters. These clusters are more general conceptual groupings of the original set of statements. Finally, average ratings are computed for each statement and for each cluster.

Step 5: Interpreting the Maps

To interpret the conceptualization, we assemble certain materials and follow a specific sequence of steps—a process that has been developed on the basis of our experiences with many different projects. The materials consist of the original statements and clusters, a series of maps depicting these statements and clusters as well as related variable data, and rating comparison graphs known as pattern matches and go-zones. These materials start with the following:

1. *The Statement List.* The original list of brainstormed statements; each item is shown with an identifying number.
2. *The Cluster List.* A listing of the statements as they were grouped into clusters by the cluster analysis.

Next, there is a series of maps:

3. *The Point Map.* A map that shows the statements as they were placed by multi-dimensional scaling.
4. *The Cluster Map.* A map that shows how statements were grouped by the cluster analysis.
5. *The Point Rating Map.* The numbered point map with average statement ratings overlaid.
6. *The Cluster Rating Map.* The cluster map with average cluster ratings overlaid.

Notice that there are several different types of maps here. Which of them is *the* concept map? In fact, they are all concept maps. Each of these maps tells us something about the major ideas and how they are interrelated. Each emphasizes a different aspect of the conceptual information. Two additional displays facilitate comparison of the rating results across different criteria:

7. *Pattern Matches.* Pairwise comparisons of cluster ratings across criteria such as different stakeholder groups, rating variables, or points in time, using a ladder graph representation. The structure and use of these graphs are described later in this chapter.
8. *Go-Zones.* Bivariate graphs of statement values for two rating variables within a cluster, divided into quadrants above and below the mean of each variable, showing a "go-zone" quadrant of statements that are above average on both variables.

Although these maps and graphs are distinctly different ways of portraying or representing the conceptual structure, it is important to remember that they are all interrelated and simply reflect different views of the same phenomenon.

Interpretation involves distributing the materials in sequence to the participant group and directing certain interpretive tasks such as examining and naming clusters of statements.

Step 6: Utilization

At this point, the group discusses ways to use the final concept maps, pattern matches, and go-zones to enhance either planning or evaluation. The uses of these tools are limited only by the creativity and motivation of the group. For planning, these results might be used for structuring the subsequent planning effort or as the framework for an outline of a planning report. In evaluation, the concept map, pattern matching, and go-zones can act as an organizing device for operationalizing and implementing the program, as a guide for measurement development, or as a framework for examining patterns of outcomes.

How Concept Mapping Works: An Example

To illustrate how the concept mapping process works, we consider here a hypothetical, decontextualized example that shows each step in the process. Each of the remaining chapters concentrates on a specific step of the process in considerable detail and shows numerous examples of real-world projects to illustrate some of the issues and variations involved in concept mapping.

Imagine a situation where a local organization that serves the community is involved in a planning process to determine its future priorities and decides to use the concept mapping methodology to help accomplish this. First, at the preparation stage, the organizers would discuss desired results of the initiative, identify groups of stakeholders, and generate the *focus statements*—specifically, a brainstorming focus statement and focus prompt designed to elicit ideas about the topic of interest and one or more rating focus statements for rating the statements on characteristics of interest. A typical brainstorming focus statement might look like this:

"Generate statements that describe specific services that our agency should provide to its community in order to address our organizational mission."

This might then be translated into a focus prompt:

"One service that our agency should provide in the future in order to address our organizational mission is . . ."

A typical rating focus statement might be as follows:

"Rate the importance of each statement on a scale from '1' to '5,' where '1' equals
the lowest level of importance and '5' equals the highest level of importance."

At the next stage, generation of ideas and issues, a brainstorming process is
conducted (using the brainstorming focus prompt defined earlier) to generate
statements. For example, statements in response to the above prompt might
include the following:

1. Employee assistance programs

2. Outpatient services for the elderly

3. Foster parent training

At this point, collected statements are processed to consolidate duplicate or
nonrelevant statements. If the number of brainstormed statements is suffi-
ciently large (e.g., greater than 100), the statement set may be analyzed and
edited, maintaining as much as possible the original ideas of the group within
the smaller edited set of statements.

Next, each participant sorts the statements for similarity, either manually or
using computer software, subject to the constraints discussed earlier: that each
pile cannot consist of one statement (in other words, the result cannot be a one-
to-one correspondence between number of statements and number of piles);
that all statements cannot be in a single pile, and that no statement can be in
more than one pile. Then each participant rates each statement according to the
rating focus statement(s) established earlier.

Now, the grouping and rating data are analyzed as described in Chapter 4
of this volume, using a sequence of analyses (e.g., multidimensional scaling
and cluster analysis) to produce the following results displays:

1. *Point Map.* This map (shown in Figure 1.3) is a display of the two-
dimensional multidimensional scaling of the grouping data, showing points
corresponding to each statement. The proximity of these statement points is
based on which statements were more likely to have been placed in the same
pile by the participants.

In the map shown, the points for statements 10 and 76 on the left are physically
close to each other. This indicates that these statements were more likely to have
been grouped together in the same pile by the participants. For example, in a public
health planning study, the following statements would be likely to be grouped
together by most sorters under a category of "Working With Providers":

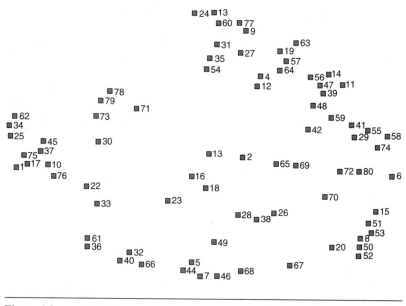

Figure 1.3   Point Map

Statement 10: "Educate providers about community beliefs towards preventive health screening."

Statement 76: "Work with providers to increase understanding and buy-in for existing screening guidelines and practices."

The point map is a *relational* map, in that it shows the statements in relation to each other. The orientation of the map is not important to the analysis of the results—this map could be rotated clockwise or counterclockwise or flipped horizontally or vertically and the points would still have the same positions relative to each other. This map often serves as a discussion tool for participants to explore the relationship among statements and to start to define categories for proximate groups of statements.

2. *Point Cluster Map.* A point cluster map represents the overlaying of the hierarchical cluster analysis results onto the original multidimensional scaling point map, as shown in Figure 1.4. The cluster analysis groups related statements into discrete groupings, represented by two-dimensional polygons. This map is useful in relating each cluster to its relevant statements and for asking

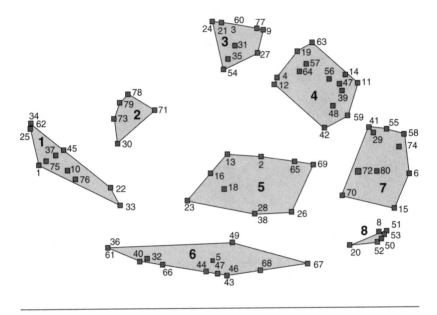

Figure 1.4   Point Cluster Map

participants to suggest appropriate labels for the clusters. For example, in a community mental health planning study, the statements in cluster 1 on the left might all be about educational outreach efforts, whereas the larger cluster 4 on the right may contain statements about outpatient treatment options.

Note that the polygon shapes of the clusters are produced by joining the outermost points in each cluster as determined by the analysis. Regarding the size of the clusters, broader cluster shapes usually represent broader concepts, whereas more compact clusters generally represent more narrowly focused concepts. In the sample figure above and in subsequent cluster maps shown in this introductory example, the clusters are shown using placeholder labels of 1, 2, 3, and so forth. In an actual study, some or all of the stakeholders would be involved in a process of labeling these clusters with descriptive labels such as "Education" or "Outpatient Services," in ways that make the most sense to them. These labels, in turn, represent a key summary of the domain of ideas generated by the brainstorming process. Actual examples of maps provided throughout this volume show clusters with stakeholder-authored labels.

3. *Cluster Map.* The cluster map displays the labeled results of the cluster analysis and provides a "big picture" overview of the domain of ideas. Figure 1.5 shows an example of a cluster map.

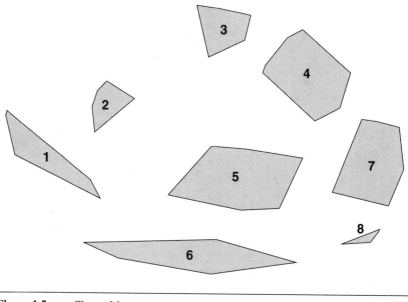

Figure 1.5   Cluster Map

Together, the point and cluster maps (Figures 1.3 through 1.5) constitute the conceptual framework generated for a study. The following two maps then simply use these structures as a framework for displaying the rating data.

4. *Point Rating Map.* A point rating map overlays the point map with a graphical representation of the rating priorities that have been averaged for each statement. Figure 1.6 shows an example of a point rating map.

In this map, the number of "blocks" in a column's height indicates the average relative importance for each statement, according to the stakeholders who contributed rating input. In this figure, for example, it is visibly apparent that the items of highest importance tended to fall in the eastern or northeastern portions of the map.

5. *Cluster Rating Map.* In a cluster rating map, the average rating values are computed for each cluster of statements and displayed as a third dimension on top of the cluster map. As with the point rating map, clusters with higher values in the third dimension contain statements that participants gave higher

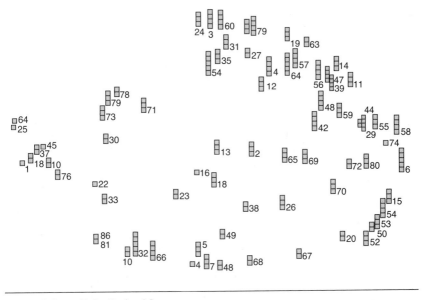

Figure 1.6 Point Rating Map

average ratings. Figure 1.7 shows an example of a cluster rating map. The relative heights of each cluster indicate the relative importance of each group of ideas compared to the others on the map.

Thus far, we have computed maps showing the statement domain in the form of their proximity (via the multidimensional scaling analysis), their clusters (via the cluster analysis), and average statement ratings relative to these points and clusters. However, an important part of the planning and evaluation process is the comparison of these results across multiple variables, subgroups, or over time. Two additional kinds of displays, known as *pattern matches* and *go-zone* displays, are designed specifically to address this.

6. *Pattern Matches.* A pattern matching display provides a comparison of average cluster ratings between two variables, such as

- Between two separate stakeholder groups
- Between two different rating variables, such as impact and feasibility
- Across different points in time

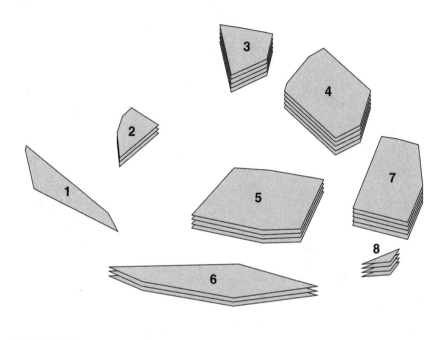

Figure 1.7   Cluster Rating Map

A pattern matching display uses a "ladder graph" representation of the data, so named because a perfect correlation between the two *patterns* would display as straight lines between all clusters, like rungs on a ladder (see Figure 1.8). The display is constructed as follows:

1. The analysis computes averages across participants to arrive at a statement average and then computes averages across all statements within a cluster to arrive at a cluster average on the scale in question.

2. One variable is shown on each side, and clusters are listed on each side in the order that they are rated according to this variable by the participant group.

3. The position of each cluster on the ladder graph is based on its rating value for the variable in question.

4. Straight lines are drawn between the same cluster on each side of the graph. The data can be represented by color-coded, dashed, or grayscale lines that link

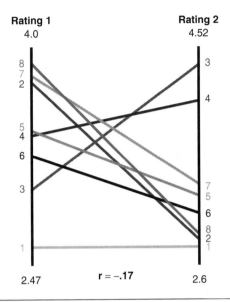

Figure 1.8   Pattern Matching Between Two Variables

the cluster name on the left to the same cluster name on the right for ease of viewing.

5. A correlational value known as the Pearson product-moment correlation, representing the relationship between the two variables, is displayed at the bottom of the graph.

Recall that each line on this pattern match represents a group of ideas that are now represented as a cluster.

Some of the variables that can be reviewed via pattern matching include the following:

• Comparison of two rating variables, such as the importance versus feasibility of statement clusters. Such comparisons can provide valuable guidance to the planning and evaluation process, as in the case where stakeholders see difficulties in implementing a desired outcome or do not value some solutions as highly as others.

• Results of a specific variable between two separate stakeholder groups. For example, a concept mapping effort for a public health study may show that stakeholders from the medical community value research efforts most highly, whereas stakeholders from the aging community may place a much higher value on caregiver support services.

• Comparison of a variable over time, such as the importance ratings of statement clusters during the planning versus evaluation stages of a project.

In Figure 1.8, the average cluster ratings have a relatively low correlation across the two variables shown, as evidenced by both the low Pearson product-moment correlation of -0.17 and the wide divergence between cluster rating values on either side. As can be seen on the graph, cluster 1 compares very closely across both variables, being low on average for both, whereas clusters 4 and 6 have moderately different ratings and other clusters have very divergent average ratings.

Within a study, pattern matching represents an important technique for understanding the divergence of opinion between different stakeholder groups, rating variables, points in time, or other criteria, as a means of discussing these differences and understanding their impact on the goals of the study.

7. *Go-Zones.* The third major concept mapping graphic, in addition to the maps and pattern matches, is known as a "go-zone" graph. A go-zone is a specific type of bivariate plot of the data in a pattern match, generally showing the averages for each statement within a cluster. It plots the statement results in an $X–Y$ graph, divided in quadrants above and below the mean value within the cluster of each rating variable. Figure 1.9 shows a go-zone display.

The vertical line describes the mean of the values in this cluster on the X axis, and the horizontal line describes the mean of the values in this cluster on the Y axis, thus dividing cluster contents into four quadrants.

The term go-zone springs from the fact that upper-right quadrant displays statements of a cluster that were rated above average on both variables. In many situations, these will represent the most actionable statements within the cluster. This upper-right quadrant contains statements that were ranked above the mean for both variables—for example, those statements that are rated above the average in both importance and feasibility, and would thus indicate a higher implementation priority.

The other quadrants provide important feedback as well. In this example, presuming that the X axis describes importance and the Y axis describes feasibility, the upper-left quadrant would contain statements that are higher on average in feasibility but lower in importance, indicating a lower priority from the stakeholders. Similarly, the lower-right quadrant would contain statements with higher

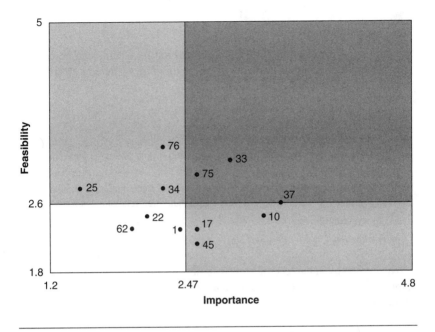

Figure 1.9   A Go-Zone Display Comparing Statements Across Two Rating
Criteria

importance but lower feasibility, indicating challenges for implementation. Finally, the lower-left quadrant would identify statements that are below average in both importance and feasibility, indicating a lower priority for implementation.

The example shown in Figure 1.9 uses different shading colors to clearly differentiate a white zone of statements below both mean values, lightly shaded zones of statements that are rated above the mean for only one variable, and a darker shaded go-zone of statement above the mean for both rating variables. In the case in which these variables were to represent importance and feasibility, as described above, the statements within the shaded quadrant would represent the most likely initial targets for action within the cluster.

Once these maps and graphs are distributed to the participant groups and interpreted, the study can then progress to the utilization phase, in which the representation of ideas can become a framework for action. The facilitator normally guides this process, with the planning or evaluation outcomes driven by the participant group's interpretation of the results.

SUMMARY

The group concept mapping process described in this volume can be used to help develop a conceptual framework for planning or evaluation efforts. The process involves a series of six major steps:

1. Preparing for concept mapping
2. Generating the ideas, usually through brainstorming
3. Structuring the statements, usually through grouping the statements into piles and rating each one
4. Concept mapping analysis, representing ideas in maps that are computed using a combination of multidimensional scaling and hierarchical cluster analysis
5. Interpreting the maps
6. Utilization

The remaining chapters of this volume describe in detail how concept mapping processes like these can be constructed and used in planning or evaluation contexts.

EXERCISES

1. Together with others in a small group, brainstorm and write down as many different conceptualization situations as you can think of in a few minutes. Classify these into the following categories: operational planning, strategic planning, process evaluation, outcome evaluation, and other. For the others, come up with a simple classification scheme.

2. For one of the conceptualization situations you brainstormed for Exercise 1, or for some other situation of your own choosing, begin to outline how you would set up a concept mapping process. Write brief answers for each of the following:

   a. What type of conceptualization situation is this (e.g., operational planning, outcome evaluation)?

   b. What is the purpose of the concept mapping in this case?

   c. Is concept mapping justified in this case, or could a conceptual framework be readily devised using some other process?

   d. Who are the likely and/or desirable participants in this concept mapping project?

   e. Are there any factors you're aware of that might interfere with or jeopardize the concept mapping process?

   - Are the participants likely to be motivated? By what? What stake do participants have in the outcome?

   - Are there political and/or interpersonal tensions that might affect the process?

   - Does the organization have the motivational and financial resources to support the concept mapping and subsequent activities?

   - What are the possible "hidden agendas" that might be motivating this project?

2

Preparing for Concept Mapping

> Well begun is half done.
> —Aristotle, quoting an old proverb

This chapter describes how to prepare for a concept mapping process. It examines some of the important issues that arise at the very start of any concept mapping process; particularly important are the selection of the facilitator and the nature of the initiator(s)-facilitator relationship. It also looks at the development of the focus, selection of the participants, determination of methods to be used, and negotiation of a schedule, communication plan, and resources. Finally, a questionnaire to help develop a written plan will be presented to summarize the preparation issues discussed.

Preparation is the most important step in the concept mapping process because thoughtful decisions at this stage will help ensure a smooth and meaningful process, and errors made here may be amplified as the process unfolds. Before discussing specific preparations to make, let's consider how a concept mapping process typically originates. Figure 2.1 shows a flowchart describing the steps that are typically followed in planning for concept mapping.

The preparation stage involves several tasks:

- *Define the Issue.* Identify the core need, interest, or issue to be examined.
- *Initiate the Process.* Define the need for a concept mapping project and move it forward as appropriate, driven by the goals and desired outcomes, through initiator(s) who may be either an individual or a team put together to ensure both political and practical coverage for the project.
- *Select the Facilitator.* Choose a person outside or inside the organization who will facilitate and enable the process.
- *Determine Goals and Purposes.* Identify the goals and desired outcomes of the concept mapping project.
- *Define the Focus.* Discuss the goal and the focus of the concept mapping.
- *Select the Participants.* Choose the people who will participate in the concept mapping, informed by goals and purposes, as well as the resulting focus statements.
- *Determine Participation Methods.* Identify whether goals of the process are best served using on-site versus remote brainstorming, sorting, and rating, as well as appropriate stakeholder group sizes for each step.

Preparation

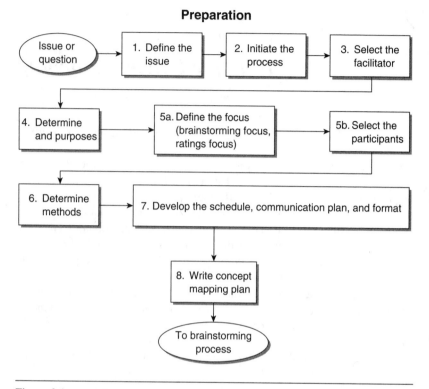

Figure 2.1   A Flowchart for Preparing a Concept Mapping Process

- *Develop the Schedule, Communication Plan, and Format.* Establish the time frame for the steps of the concept mapping process, the plan for communicating these steps to participants, and the best format for the final reports, presentations, or publications.
- *Determine Resources.* Clarify the resources and budget of the process.
- *Get Human Subjects Approval.* In many institutions it is a requirement that all data collection involving human subjects be approved by an Institutional Review Board (IRB).
- *Write Concept Mapping Plan.* These preparatory steps should result in a written plan describing the concept mapping process.

The resulting document can be a contract or a less formal description of the overall plan. This plan is generally written by the initiator after consulting with the potential participants. It should ensure that participants know what topic they are conceptualizing and why the process is being undertaken, discuss logistical issues and scheduling, and allow for maximum participation and sufficient time to do a high-quality job.

DEFINE THE ISSUE

Concept mapping projects generally spring from a specified need or interest, one that requires participatory input from a broad range of stakeholders to understand, plan action, and evaluate. In the social sciences, for example, such issues could include the following:

- What actions would most effectively improve a specific area of public health?
- How can agencies make the most effective use of organizational resources?
- What are the best uses of limited public funds for solving social issues?
- What are core areas that should be addressed in strategic planning for long-range goals?
- What are the most important evaluation criteria for program effectiveness?

Later in the process, these issues are used to develop specific *focus statements* used to generate and/or rate ideas in support of them. At this point, however, the more important task is to define the issues themselves and review how a concept mapping process can help create outcomes in support of them.

INITIATE THE PROCESS

Most concept mapping processes begin with a need, interest, or issue within an organization or group. For example, the director of the organization or department may decide to begin a long-range planning process, or the head of a social program or the agency responsible for its oversight may decide that a program requires evaluation. The first stage of this process is to determine the scope that this project should encompass and determine its strategic focus. It is also at this stage that the key stakeholders of a concept mapping process start to be identified, including the following participants:

- *Initiator(s).* The person or persons responsible for starting the concept mapping process. They hold the ultimate responsibility for a project and for determining the best course of action for it.

- *Facilitator(s)*. The person or persons who will actually supervise the concept mapping process.

- *Advisory Group*. A subset of the larger stakeholder group who is tasked with an oversight and advisory role for some or all phases of the project.

- *Core Participant Group*. A representative group of stakeholders who will commit to being involved in all phases of a concept mapping project, including brainstorming, idea synthesis, sorting, rating, and analysis.

- *Invited Participant Group*. A broad group of stakeholders at all levels of involvement with an issue, including representatives across all dimensions of the stakeholder base, e.g., front-line to leadership, public to private sector, research to practice, acute care to public health, etc.

It is important to note that the scope of a project is not always predetermined, and the issues that originally present themselves to the initiators may in fact point to deeper ones with time and further discussion—for example, what may seem to be an issue with the health behaviors of a specific population group might, in fact, reflect larger issues in their social context or generalize to other groups. Ideally, initiators should keep an open mind as they launch a project, and should work with their chosen facilitator to determine an appropriate project scope that addresses their needs.

SELECT THE FACILITATOR

As one of the first steps in the process, the initiators will select or identify the person or team who will serve as the facilitators. Sometimes, the process is conducted entirely within the organization, and the facilitator is one of the organization's staff members. In other situations, the organization may not have someone internally who can act as facilitator or the organization would prefer to have an outside consultant fulfill that role.

The initiators must first decide whether to have internal or external facilitators, and they will consider the tradeoffs involved in the choice between internal facilitators and resources from outside the organization. An internal facilitator is likely to be known by some or all of the participants, and may have knowledge of the organization and the issue at hand that will contribute to the effort in a positive way. It's also likely that an internal facilitator will be able to work more effectively with participants' time constraints and accomplish the activities of the project without demanding additional participant time outside of normal work hours. In a politically or interpersonally charged environment, however, the participants may not be as cooperative with or supportive of someone they know, creating more suspicion about the process, the facilitator's ability to influence it, or even his or her ability to handle the process correctly. On the other hand, an external facilitator has the appearance of impartiality and objectivity and may also possess a level of subject expertise not readily available in the organization. If he or she is well known and respected in the field or by members of the organization, the participants may accept the process more readily from the outset. Using an external facilitator may also imply that the organization is more strongly committed to the process because it was willing to provide additional funding for the project.

Certain types of facilitators can be better for certain types of projects. An internal facilitator might be better for operational planning or process evaluation, because both of these focus on a detailed examination of the internal day-to-day functioning of some part of the organization; the internal facilitator would more likely be familiar with such details. An external facilitator might be more appropriate for strategic planning or outcome evaluations where the focus is much broader and less dependent on internal details, and where the organization may be more threatened by the results or implications of the process. Similarly, an external facilitator can bring an outside perspective that, in turn, can more accurately define the overall scope of the project.

The first decisions that the facilitator and initiator make together are also the most important to the outcome: what is the focus of this concept mapping project, and who will participate in the different stages of this process? The initiator and facilitator may have very different perspectives. The initiator is probably a manager and, as such, may require a timely, efficient, and logistically manageable process to meet a defined objective. The facilitator (especially if external) may wish to explore issues that may not have been clearly articulated by the initiators, and will want to ensure sufficient breadth of opinion to yield a thorough concept mapping, as well as sufficient time to interpret fully and understand the results. Therefore, the initiator may suggest a predetermined focus statement, fewer participants, more internal participants (because they are easier to schedule), fewer and shorter sessions, and so on. Conversely, the facilitator may wish to explore focus issues in more depth and argue for broader participation, more sessions, and more time within each session. Here, the facilitator has an important role in probing needs as well as practical aspects to ensure that desired outcomes are surfaced and articulated and to help guide the best design of a project given its needs, constraints, and time frame.

There are no simple, hard-and-fast rules for deciding these issues, and the initiator and facilitator usually arrive at a reasonable consensus through the planning discussions, enabling an exploration of perspectives and needs. In these discussions, it is important for the facilitator to point out some of the trade-offs discussed above and present various options for consideration.

DEVELOP THE GOALS AND THE PURPOSES

The initiators and facilitator in a particular study should agree about the general goal or purpose of the concept mapping before moving forward with detailed planning for it. Concept mapping is a method and technique applied to serve some larger purpose—it is a means to an end. Thus, the motivating factors for undertaking the study at hand dictate the goals and design of the process. In strategic planning contexts, using the concept mapping study design can help bring to the surface the major issues that are perceived to be important, usually over a long-term period. In operational planning, it can provide a framework for the construction of some specific program or activity (e.g., a training curriculum). For process evaluation, concept mapping can provide a structure for developing measures or observations of the process. For outcome evaluations, it could outline the major constructs to measure or the outcomes to be expected (we will discuss all of these in greater detail in later chapters). When discussing and arriving at agreement on the goals and focus of the project, the facilitator often assists the initiators to determine the best method of communicating the need for and potential value of this endeavor, as well as the value of their contributions to it. These specific goals and purposes—informed by the initiating need or interest— become the basis for selecting specific focus statements for brainstorming and rating, as well as appropriate stakeholder groups that must be subsequently represented in the process.

DEFINE THE FOCUS

Once the goal or goals have been clarified, the next step is the formulation of the focus, or domain, of the conceptualization. In the typical project, two separate and specific products need to be developed: the focus statement for the *brainstorming* session and the focus statements for any statement *rating*.

The focus for both the brainstorming and the ratings should be worded as specific instructions, so that all of the participants can agree in advance on the task. In developing the focus statements for both brainstorming and rating, the facilitator usually meets with the participants or some representative subgroup, discusses various alternatives for wording each focus, and attempts to reach a group consensus on final choices. For example:

- A brainstorming focus in a strategic planning process might be worded "Generate short phrases or sentences that describe specific services that your organization might provide."

- In a *needs assessment,* a focus prompt might state "A specific capability that your counselors must be able to demonstrate in their work with clients is . . . "
- Similarly, a rating focus for a program evaluation might be worded "Rate each potential outcome on a seven-point scale in terms of how strongly you think it will be affected by the program, where '1' means 'Not at all affected,' '4' means 'Moderately affected,' and '7' means 'Extremely affected.'"

The group should agree on the specific wording for each of these focus statements. These are described in more detail below.

The first focus statement, the *brainstorming focus,* serves to elicit the pool of participant ideas to be analyzed for the study. For any brainstorming session, the focus can be stated in a variety of ways. In strategic planning, participants might focus on the goals of the organization, the mission of the organization, or the activities or services that the organization might provide. Similarly, in program evaluations they might focus on the nature of the program, the outcomes they would like to measure, or the types of people to include in the evaluation.

When defining the brainstorming focus, it is helpful to anticipate the kinds of statements likely to be generated. Double-barreled focus statements may send very confusing messages to the participants. For example, if the statement reads "Generate short statements or sentences that describe the goals of our organization and the needs of our clients," participants may perceive these two categories as particularly distinct and sort them as two major clusters on the final concept map. As a result, some of the finer relationships that might be of interest would probably be obscured (Keith, 1989). If both emphases are important, the organization should conduct two separate conceptualizations— or, perhaps more importantly, conduct a preliminary needs analysis that helps define the most appropriate focus for this study.

This does not preclude using multiple terms in the focus statement where it is appropriate to the goals of the study. In one study (Trochim, 1989c) addressing the needs of the elderly in a county, for example, the brainstorming focus was a broad one: "Generate statements that describe the issues, problems, concerns, or needs that the elderly in our county have." Although this seems to violate the advice on avoiding double-barreled statements, participants felt that "issues, problems, concerns, or needs" were similar and would lead to a relatively homogeneous group of brainstormed statements.

Once a single focus concept has been established, how should the focus statement be worded? The answer is "It depends." Here are two common forms:

- *The statement form* takes the form of a statement instruction, such as "Generate statements about (a specific issue)" or "Generate ideas about (a specific issue)."

- *The prompt form* uses an incomplete sentence designed to lead people to answer it, such as "A specific idea for this issue would be . . . " or "The best approach for this problem would be . . . " This form is generally preferred, because it tends to produce responses that are easier for the facilitator and team to work with. In taking advantage of the natural tendency for people to complete sentences, this form is more likely to yield ideas that are syntactically similar, thus keeping the emphasis on the content of the ideas.

No matter what form the focus statement ultimately takes, it is important to "pilot test" the focus with a preliminary group of people, such as committee members for the study or a test group, to see how effective it will be at generating ideas for subsequent analysis. This pilot test will reveal whether the focus statement elicits an appropriate quantity and quality of responses. More importantly, it is a needed "quality assurance" check to make sure that participants accurately understand the intent of this focus and generate responses that are germane to the study. For example, a workplace performance study may initially have a prompt of "The best way to improve our organization is . . . "—but rather than generating ideas on improving performance, a pilot study may reveal that it instead elicits responses that focus solely on working conditions. This pilot test ultimately serves as a preliminary sample of how the larger group of stakeholders will respond to the prompt.

Once the brainstorming focus is developed, one or more *rating focus* statements must be defined for participants to provide comparative ratings for the ideas generated. Here, as with the brainstorming focus statement, form should follow function: one should consider how the resulting information will be used. A conceptualization for planning might ask participants to rate how important each brainstormed item is, or how much emphasis should be placed upon it in the planning process. In evaluation, one might ask them to rate how much effort should be given to various program components, or how much they believe each outcome is likely to be affected by the program.

In the services for the elderly study (Trochim, 1989c) mentioned above, the rating focus statement was "Rate each statement on a 1 to 5 scale for how much priority it should be given in the planning process, where '1' equals the lowest priority and '5' equals the highest priority."

The reader might wish to consult the literature on how to focus and develop questions for measurement and surveys (Fowler, 2001) to gain further insight into wording issues relevant to brainstorming and rating foci.

SELECT THE PARTICIPANTS

Participants and focus go hand in hand when designing a concept mapping initiative. The focus statement is of course driven by the goals and desired outcomes of this endeavor; this leads logically to the observation that the goals and desired outcomes are for the purpose of changing, innovating, or adding to knowledge. The participants, then, are to be identified and selected to enable change, create and adopt innovation, or add to knowledge.

Once these focus statements have been defined, these can in turn inform discussions between the initiators and facilitator regarding which stakeholders should participate in the concept mapping project. This discussion should be guided by the nature of the task and an awareness of the respective roles of the facilitator and initiator. For an operational planning model—say, a specific function within a specific department—it may make sense to include targeted and knowledgeable participants from within the agency. For strategic planning or outcome evaluation, a broad range of experience and input is perfectly appropriate, including wide participation from within the organization and the engagement of knowledgeable, committed, or potentially affected persons from outside (e.g., members of the board, client groups, or political bodies).

In general, a conceptualization is best when it includes a wide variety of relevant people. For example, if one is conducting strategic planning for a human services organization, with a brainstorming focus revolving around future needs or programs, participants might include administrative staff, service staff, board members, clients, and relevant members of community groups. In a program evaluation context, one might similarly include administrators, program staff, clients, social science theorists, community members, and relevant funding agent representatives. Broad, heterogeneous participation helps to ensure the consideration of a wide variety of viewpoints; provides more information for the statistical analyses, thus improving the clarity and resolution of the maps; and encourages a broader range of people to "buy into" the resulting conceptual framework. Depending on the specific project, there may also be political advantages to being able to say that broad participation was possible, even if people don't take advantage of that opportunity.

In some situations, however, the authors have used relatively small homogeneous groups for the conceptualization process. For instance, an organization that is beginning an operational planning effort and would like quickly to lay out some of its major concepts might prefer to use a relatively small group of administrators and organizational staff members. An obvious advantage of this is that it is logistically simpler to get people together for meetings if they are all on the staff of the organization. A group like this works well when a quick conceptualization framework is desired, but in general we would recommend a broader sampling of opinion.

Number of Participants

There is no strict limit on the number of people who can participate in concept mapping. Although initially designed for use with live groups of 40 or fewer people, it is now frequently used with very large, geographically dispersed groups using tools such as the Internet. In general, having more participants yields greater amounts of information to be used in the analyses and, consequently, produces greater resolution and clarity of the results, although there are likely to be diminishing returns (Trochim, 1993) as sample size increases beyond a certain point. Scheduling becomes an issue in the case of live single-site concept mapping efforts: involving more people usually makes it difficult to schedule sessions that everyone can attend and imposes constraints on the extent to which the group discussions can involve everyone. Typically, 40 or fewer participate in such studies, with a minimum of 10 people, although exceptions to this are possible; this range seems to provide a good framework, ensuring a variety of opinions while still enabling good group discussion and interpretation.

The Sampling Plan for Participant Selection

In some cases, the initiators and facilitator can simply directly identify the people who will participate in the concept mapping. In other cases, they may specify the *kinds* of people they would like represented, and the facilitator will devise a sampling plan for selecting them.

As in all sampling situations, a key decision is whether the sampling procedure (Trochim, 2001) will be random (e.g., probabilistic) or nonrandom. In some contexts, it might be reasonable to use some random sampling scheme to select participants from a larger defined population. This is most useful if the resulting concept map is to be generalizable to the population of interest. Simple random sampling schemes, of course, run the risk of underrepresenting minority groups from the population, and so, if sampling is used, it will typically be best to attempt some form of stratified random sampling where we deliberately oversample subgroups that have small percentages in the population of interest.

Random sampling will not always be practical or desirable. The goal is to achieve a broad sampling of *ideas* rather than a representative sampling of persons. So, it is usually preferable to do purposive sampling for heterogeneity—that is, to nonrandomly select a broad range of persons who are likely to reflect the full spectrum of ideas that are relevant for the concept mapping process.

There are also sample-size implications for different phases of a concept mapping project, depending on whether you are approaching the concept mapping project with a "focus group" or "survey research" frame of mind. If the former, then smaller sample sizes are sufficient. If the latter, more structured sampling of stakeholder groups is warranted. In many of our projects, we take the development of the map itself, e.g., the sorting or cluster interpretation phases, as a type of focus group and use a small heterogeneous sampling approach, whereas for ratings we take something closer to a survey model and sample more formally or invite the entire population.

Ultimately, a clearly written sampling plan should be developed and agreed to by both the initiators and facilitator. This written sampling plan, or a written list of selected individuals, constitutes part of the concept mapping plan and schedule.

DETERMINE PARTICIPATION METHODS

Concept mapping is adaptable to a wide range of group formats. It can be used with small meetings or large professional workshops or scaled upwards to include thousands of people worldwide over the Internet, with every variation in between. The methods of participation that are used follow from the goals, focus statements, and participant population of a study, and involve the following options.

Brainstorming Activity

The brainstorming process (Adams, 1979; Osborn, 1948) can be performed in a live group setting, remotely via the Internet, or through other media such as mail, fax, or direct participant contact. Less commonly, concept mapping studies have even been performed with no active participant input whatsoever, by analyzing words or statements in a database. Your choice of brainstorming methodology will be driven by the purpose of the study and influenced by factors such as the availability of participants, their geographic locations and ability to travel, the time required, and the desirability of having participants interact with each other as part of the brainstorming process. A considerable literature (Collaros & Lynn, 1969; Diehl & Wolfgang, 1987, 1991; Jablin, 1981; Valacich & Nunamaker, 1992) has developed on the conditions that enhance brainstorming productivity and the factors that might inhibit productivity and quality. In general, this literature suggests that there is considerable value in small face-to-face groups and in using Internet technology as a means for brainstorming.

Sorting and Rating Activities

Concept mapping is most commonly conducted with all who participated in the brainstorming activity above also participating in the structuring steps; i.e., the sorting and rating activities. In recent years, concept mapping projects have grown in participant population to include hundreds, so it is not always practical or desirable to include all participants in all steps. Deciding on the participation for the sorting and rating steps of a concept mapping process involves two issues:

- The first is whether all participants will participate in the process, as might be the case in a smaller group, or whether a subset of the participant population will perform these operations. Commonly, when large participant populations are involved, a core group of key stakeholders is identified for the sorting and rating activities.

- The second issue is how to physically perform the sorting and rating activities, with similar choices as for the brainstorming process: a live meeting, remote sorting and rating via the Internet, mail, or fax, or some combination of the two.

The facilitator should present options for participation levels or methods to the initiators, who will be most familiar with people and resources involved, and negotiate a strategy that makes the most sense for the study.

DEVELOP THE SCHEDULE, COMMUNICATION PLAN, AND FORMAT

As part of the initial meeting between the initiators and facilitator, the parties should develop a plan for the infrastructure of the concept mapping effort, including the following:

- A written schedule for the concept mapping process
- A plan for communicating responsibilities and time frames within this schedule to affected parties
- The format for the completed project deliverables

The schedule will depend in large part on the availability of the participants and the time the facilitator has to accomplish the necessary mapping work. No schedule will work well in every situation—each activity must be tailored to the specific needs of the project. Two hypothetical scenarios are presented here to illustrate some of the trade-offs involved in scheduling decisions, where it is assumed that the participants and focus have already been negotiated. Both presume a live concept mapping process involving a single group of people, and are designed to work best with around 20 or fewer participants; by comparison, remote concept mapping processes using the Internet may take place over a period ranging from weeks to months, to allow people to take part asynchronously.

Schedule 1: Three Weekly Meetings

This schedule is the most leisurely. It allocates sufficient time for the group process at each of the three steps and provides generous analysis time for the facilitator. The sample schedule given below assumes three sessions held on successive Mondays in a setting such as a staff or group meeting. Such a schedule might be appropriate—as is or with some modifications—for community groups responsible for planning for human services, because such groups usually meet in the evenings and it is often desirable to keep the meetings relatively short.

- *First Monday.* Generation of statements (facilitator will generate cards and rating sheets before the second meeting)—one hour
- *Second Monday.* Structuring of statements—for grouping and rating of statements (facilitator will conduct analysis and prepare interpretation materials before the third meeting)—90 minutes
- *Third Monday.* Interpretation of maps—to interpret maps and decide how they will be used—two hours

This is by far the more generous of the two schedules; it should provide ample time for accomplishing a high-quality concept mapping process. This "slow track" has the advantage of an orderly focused process, because each of the three major steps is alloted its own time.

There are several disadvantages to this schedule. Even this apparently generous schedule will probably have some tight spots. Restricting the interpretation and utilization session to two hours may require the facilitator to cut discussion short in order to complete the job. Also, longer intervals between sessions may prompt feelings that the process is disjointed or isn't getting anywhere. Participants may also forget more of what went on in the previous sessions or lose track of where they are in the overall process. To compensate for this, the facilitator may need to spend a little time at the beginning and end of each session reorienting the participants. A practical problem with this approach is that it requires participation in three separate sessions, a probable imposition on participants' already busy schedules (although if participants are staff members of the organization, this is likely to be less of a problem than with a heterogeneous group where some members may have to travel). Finally, some fixed costs may be higher with this scheduling option. For instance, if refreshments are served or the cost of the room is by the day, this three-session schedule will obviously be more expensive.

At the same time, the slow track has some key advantages. Such a schedule may fit in well for a group that already has regularly scheduled weekly or monthly meetings. It allows the participants a great deal of time to think about the process and what they are trying to achieve. Equally important, it allows the analyst ample time to conduct the analysis and prepare high-quality materials for the interpretation session.

Schedule 2: Two Concentrated Sessions

Some of the advantages of the previous schedule can be combined with a faster pace by devising a two-session concept mapping process. In addition to being faster, such a concentrated schedule can fit very well within the structure of a retreat or "issue summit" surrounding a particular need or issue. Here, the generation and structuring steps are done on the same day, with the interpretation accomplished in a second session. The sample schedule given below shows an example of two sessions being held one week apart, with each session lasting three to five hours:

Session 1

Generation of statements: 75 minutes

Break: Minimum of two hours, to allow statement reduction and preparation

Structuring of statements: 75 minutes .

Session 2

Interpretation of maps: 90 minutes

Break: 30 minutes

Utilization and wrap-up: One hour

Practically speaking, this schedule provides stronger continuity than the three-meeting plan. Participants are more likely to understand the process sequence, and the schedule is more efficient and less costly than a three-session one.

The major disadvantage of this schedule is that the first session is cramped. If a group numbers more than 20, for example, it will be very difficult to perform statement reduction and generate sorting decks and rating sheets within a two-hour period. The facilitator can do two things to ease this "crunch." First, assistance would be extremely helpful—having two people cutting or ripping up card decks speeds up the process considerably. Second, you can plan to produce the materials (i.e., card decks and rating sheets) quickly via computer. Additionally, a different way of generating brainstormed items obviates some of these concerns: instead of typing brainstormed items directly into a computer program, each participant can write each item on separate index cards while the brainstorming is going on. They can then group these hand-written cards and even write their rating directly on each card.

It should be clear that there is no single schedule that will work for every concept mapping situation. There are trade-offs between efficiency and effectiveness, cost, and timeliness. The schedule that is finally agreed upon should come out of the pre-process negotiation session, and should have the consensus support of those who will ultimately participate. In planning these sessions, one should make a distinction between the total project time and the time "on task" required from participants. In most situations, total project time is concerned with continuity, and particularly the concern that people may forget issues and ideas over too long a period of time. Conversely, the schedule must consider the important issues of respondent burden and keeping involvement levels appropriate to the participant. In situations in which a great deal of concept mapping is being done, one should also consider the risk of dealing with respondent "burnout," where too much effort is being expected from individual participants within the project time frame. A well-planned schedule should balance the needs of a reasonable project time frame with the efforts of its participants.

Once a concept mapping process has been established, the initiators and facilitator have a basis to set an overall time frame for project completion, as well as determine the best format for the final report and/or presentation. The facilitator should interview the initiators to discuss factors such as the following:

- Access to people: who will be available during the time frame of the study, and in what roles

- Desired communications, such as reports, articles or published papers

- Driving deadlines, such as professional conferences or the end of a fiscal year

Options for deliverables from the study include the following:

- *Printed Report.* A summary of the results of the concept mapping analysis, either guided by the interpretation of the core group behind the study or, much more commonly, the results of a live meeting to interpret these concept mapping results. Some time will usually be needed after the interpretation session to produce final high-quality versions of the maps (with all cluster and region names included) and to write any narrative that might be desired.

• *Live Presentation.* Most typically, a concept mapping process concludes with a meeting among some or all of the participants to discuss and interpret the results of the concept mapping analysis.

• *Internal or External Publication.* Frequently, the results of a concept mapping analysis—and their interpretation in a live meeting and/or a printed report—become synthesized in other media such as publications and Web sites. These publications include content derived from the conclusions of the study and may or may not include the original concept maps and raw data.

Commonly, the end result of a study is a final report informed by a group interpretation of the analysis results—by a group that may or may not encompass the original participants, or be a subset of them. For example, the Healthy Aging study (Chronic Disease Directors, 2003) discussed elsewhere in this volume involved brainstorming input from a geographically distributed group of experts in the field, followed by sorting and rating by a smaller core group of people, followed by presentation of the results to invited participants at a conference retreat, followed by a written report. Another very common result is a paper in a refereed journal or professional publication, often developed by the initiators in conjunction with the facilitator, based on the results of the concept mapping study (Batterham et al., 2002; Brown & Calder, 1999; Carpenter, Van Haitsma, Ruckdeschel, & Lawton, 2000; Cousins & MacDonald, 1998; Daughtry & Kunkel, 1993; DeRidder, Depla, Severens, & Malsch, 1997; Donnelly, Donnelly, & Grohman, 2000; Gurowitz, Trochim, & Kramer, 1988; Mercier, Piat, Peladeau, & Dagenais, 2000; Michalski & Cousins, 2000; Nabitz, Severens, van den Brink, & Jansen, 2001; Pammer et al., 2001; Paulson, Truscott, & Stuart, 1999; Shern, Trochim, & Lacomb, 1995; Southern, Young, Dent, Appleby, & Batterham, 2002; Stokols et al., 2003; Trochim, Cook, & Setze, 1994; Trochim, Milstein, Wood, Jackson, & Pressler, 2004; Trochim, Stillman, Clark, & Schmitt, 2003; van Nieuwenhuizen, Schene, Koeter, & Huxley, 2001; VanderWaal, Casparie, & Lako, 1996; White & Farrell, 2001; Witkin & Trochim, 1997).

DETERMINE RESOURCES

Establishing the goals, participant population, and logistics of a concept mapping project provides the data needed to estimate the resources needed to complete the project in terms of time, number of people involved, physical facilities, and funding required. The project initiators generally take primary responsibility for arranging or negotiating these resources, with the feedback and assistance of the project facilitator, particularly if he or she brings past experience in estimating accurate resource needs for similar concept mapping projects.

As with most projects, one should be generous in the estimates of time and money required—and in particular, those involved should expect to spend more time in planning a concept mapping study than in actually executing it. Resource use must then be assessed throughout the project, both to check against initial resource projections and to adjust the project scope or negotiate further resources as needed.

WRITE CONCEPT MAPPING PLAN

The concept mapping plan is the description of all of the preparatory decisions made for a mapping project. The plan is a written description of the participants, the focus statements, and the schedule. Table 2.1 consists of a short questionnaire that can be used to help develop a written plan or, when completed, could constitute the written plan itself if no narrative is desired.

SUMMARY

The quality of the concept mapping process is dependent on the quality of the preparations that are made. Because concept mapping is a group activity, great care must be taken to identify the key players and be sensitive to potential interpersonal role conflicts. The initiators—the people responsible for motivating the study—are usually one or more organizational administrators. The facilitator—the person responsible for managing the process—may be either a member of the organization or an outside consultant. In order to ensure that a wide range of opinions will be incorporated into the maps, the participants in the process should, whenever feasible, be selected from a broadly defined group of stakeholders. The participants, or some representative subgroup, should be included in the negotiations surrounding the planning of the process, including the goals and focus statements and the development of a suitable schedule. The results of this process should be a written concept mapping plan, and there should be consensus among the participants that it is feasible and appropriate.

Table 2.1
A Questionnaire to Guide the Development of a Concept Mapping Plan

---

This questionnaire asks the respondent to supply the key information that is needed to compose a concept mapping plan (in fact, this instrument could be used as the written plan if a more narrative one is not required).

The Organizational Context

Organization(s) involved in initiating or sponsoring the concept mapping process:

_____

_____

Initiator(s) of the concept mapping process:

_____

_____

Designated facilitator(s) of the concept mapping process:

_____

_____

Goals and Purpose of the Concept Mapping

The major goal(s) of the concept mapping in this context:

_____

_____

_____

_____

Broader tasks this concept mapping a part of (check any that apply):
_____ Strategic Planning
_____ Operational Planning
_____ Process Evaluation
_____ Outcome Evaluation
_____ Other (please specify: _____)

Selecting the Participants

The "ideal" population of participants is:

_____

_____

Number of participants desired: _____

How will the participants be selected: Targeted identification and invitation, sampling plan?

_____

_____

_____

Developing the Focus

Describe the process that was used to develop the focus for the concept mapping:

_____

_____

State *precisely* the focus statement for the generation step:

_____

_____

State *precisely* the focus for each rating:

_____

_____

The Concept Mapping Schedule

Fill in the following schedule for the process:

	Generation	*Structuring*	*Interpretation*
Date			
Time			
Location			
Participants			

Table 2.1 (Continued)

Management

Target date for completion of the final concept map results:

_____

_____

How will the final results of the process be presented (e.g., maps, written report)?

_____

_____

How much money has been allocated for the concept mapping process?

_____

_____

What additional resources (e.g., labor, supplies, facilities, equipment) will be supplied and by whom?

_____

_____

_____

_____

How are the results of the concept mapping going to be utilized?

_____

_____

_____

_____

EXERCISES

For a context that you are familiar with, develop a hypothetical plan for a concept mapping project. If you need to, make up a fictional concept mapping context. Using the questionnaire in Table 2.1, complete all of the required information. Examine each of the following questions:

1. What problems arose as you were developing the plan? Were the problems centered in specific areas (e.g., selecting participants, developing the schedule)?
2. What revisions would you make to the questionnaire in Table 2.1 on the basis of your experience?
3. What do you think the trade-offs or advantages might be when using other types of written plans such as a letter of agreement, narrative proposal, or formal contract?

3

Generating the Ideas

> Almost all new ideas have a certain aspect of foolishness when they are
> first produced.
>
> —Alfred North Whitehead

Once the preparations have been made, we can move to a more creative part of
the concept mapping process—the generation of the ideas. Here, "generation"
refers to any procedure that yields a set of ideas that describe the conceptual
domain of interest. Brainstorming is the most common method used in this context, so this chapter will describe brainstorming in some detail. At the end of the
chapter, we also present several alternative methods for generating statements.

Successful idea generation involves steps ranging from preparation, to the
execution of the actual group process, through to subsequent processing of
the resulting ideas. Figure 3.1 shows the basic steps in flowchart form.

These steps include the following:

- *Prepare for the Brainstorming Session.* Arranging facilities, logistics, and participation for the brainstorming process.
- *Introduce the Concept Mapping and Brainstorming Process.* Providing a clear
  overview and participation guidelines to involved stakeholders.
- *Manage the Brainstorming Session.* Ensuring a smooth flow and recording of ideas.
- *Idea Synthesis—Reduce and Edit the Statement Set.* Creating a concise and edited
  set of statements for subsequent sorting and rating.

Brainstorming (Osborn, 1948) can use any number of processes, such as a
live, on-site meeting or a remote process performed via mail, fax, or the Internet
by geographically distant stakeholders. It can be facilitated as a group process in
the manner of a focus group (Stewart & Shamdasani, 1990) or involve people
submitting individual inputs over a period of time as in the nominal group technique (Delbecq, 1975). Here are some examples of different strategies that have
been used for idea generation in the concept mapping process:

- In a concept mapping project to develop workforce competencies for psychosocial rehabilitation counselors, participants generated ideas during a 45-minute
  structured brainstorming session, as part of a two-day on-site concept mapping
  project (Trochim & Cook, 1993).

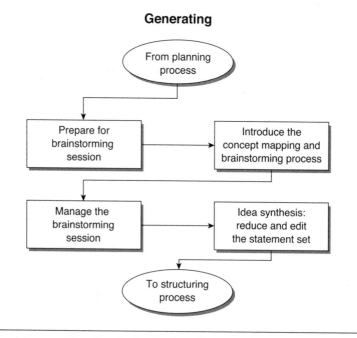

Figure 3.1   A Flowchart for Conducting a Brainstorming Session

- A state public health agency used a combination of live brainstorming meetings and remote input via the Internet to generate ideas used to define factors relating to individual tobacco use, nutrition, and physical activity, as part of an ambitious and time-critical project to define pubic health priorities to be funded from that state's share of the 1998 master settlement agreement between state governments and the tobacco industry (Trochim et al., 2004).

- A study at Cornell University looked at using written responses to an open-ended survey as input for a concept mapping process, using a survey question on norms within class project teams among a group of 76 Hotel School undergraduates (Jackson & Trochim, 2002).

PREPARE FOR THE BRAINSTORMING SESSION

First, we will look at the procedural and logistical issues in managing an on-site brainstorming session in which participants can interact with one another. Next, we'll consider issues involved with remote brainstorming, which increasingly allows very large and geographically dispersed groups of stakeholders to participate in a concept mapping process.

Preparation for On-Site Brainstorming

For situations in which stakeholders can be assembled within a single location for a time-determinate concept mapping process, an on-site brainstorming session is frequently the most efficient way to generate ideas. This approach has the advantages of group interaction, a focus on the task at hand, and the generation of ideas within a short, efficient time period. A secondary benefit is the team building through focused work as a group, which may help the project to be accepted and used later. This approach fits naturally within the format of a designated planning or evaluation meeting.

Because the brainstorming step is usually the group's introduction to the concept mapping milieu, the facilitator is naturally interested in getting the process off to a good start. Table 3.1 provides a short checklist of issues that the facilitator should anticipate when constructing an on-site brainstorming session.

Although many of the checklist items should be obvious, it is easy to overlook important preparatory steps. The quality of a concept mapping process is largely dependent on the involvement of the participants, so they should receive invitations or announcements of the brainstorming session well enough in advance to fit it into their schedules. An e-mail, phone, or mail reminder just prior to the first meeting is also appropriate.

The facilitator will decide the method for recording the group's statements. The simplest is to write the statements on a blackboard or on sheets of posted newsprint. This is easy to accomplish, and it displays all of the statements at one time for all to see. Disadvantages are that the statements will have to be copied onto a computer in order to generate the materials for grouping, and that multiple participants cannot generate statements simultaneously. Other approaches that might be considered are brainwriting (Hiltz & Turoff, 1978; Rothwell & Kazanas, 1989), Delphi methods (Linstone & Turoff, 1975), and nominal group techniques (Delbecq, 1975).

If the technology is available, the statements can be entered directly into a computer program and displayed on a large screen so all participants can see them. Although the ability to see all statements at once is limited by what the program and computer is able to display in one screen, most people can type faster than they can write. Therefore, the brainstorming session can often progress more quickly and the group can more easily recognize its accomplishment. Of course, there is the additional benefit that the statements have to be entered only once in order to generate the grouping materials.

Table 3.1

A Checklist for Preparing for a Brainstorming Session

Task	Person Assigned	Completion Date
Advance Notice		
Send invitation or announcement to all participants		
Provide participants with written background information on the project's intent, potential application, and value.		
Send follow-up reminder (by e-mail, phone, or mail)		
Recording Method		
Choose a recording method (e.g., whiteboard, newsprint, computer display)		
Make sure a backup recording method is available		
Materials		
Define an agenda for the session		
Provide an overview of the concept mapping process		
Provide an example of a concept map		
Copies of project background		
Make sure all recording materials are ready		
Setup		
Provide comfortable seating for all participants		
Provide adequate lighting and sound		
Arrange seating so all can see and participate		
Make sure the brainstorming focus statement is posted and clearly visible		
Check for special needs of participants, if any, and determine how to accommodate them in advance.		
Dry Run		
Make sure facilitator has an outline of what will be said and done		
"Pilot test" the brainstorming session		

Other recording approaches can be tried either alone or in combination. One clever and efficient way to record the brainstormed items is to have each participant write each statement on a separate index card as it is generated. Thus, they are generating them and constructing the card decks for manual-process grouping all in one step. This may save time, especially if the brainstorming and structuring are going to be accomplished in one meeting. However, the brainstorming session may take much longer if you have slow writers in the group. There may also be problems when each person writes the items if they aren't accurate or don't write legibly. There are advantages to combining features of each of these methods. If the participants are recording the statements directly onto index cards, the facilitator or an assistant might simultaneously record them on a whiteboard, newsprint, or computer. Participants can use this "master list" to check the accuracy of their own entries.

In the category of "what can go wrong, will," the facilitator must also anticipate the availability of needed equipment and, of course, possible equipment problems. A burned-out projector light or the lack of an extension cord can cause unnecessary delays and even ruin the session. Especially when more technologically based recording methods are used, it is important to have a backup procedure ready in the event of mechanical or electrical failure.

A comfortable room for the meeting will help ensure its success. To the degree possible, the facilitator should make sure that there is sufficient comfortable seating for all, that lighting and sound are adequate, and that all participants can see and hear what is going on. Because the focus statement described in the last chapter will guide the brainstorming session, this statement should be posted and clearly visible throughout the session.

If the facilitator is new to running brainstorming meetings, a "dry run" or pilot test of the session would be most appropriate. This will enable the facilitator to rehearse preparatory comments, become familiar with the setting, and learn to anticipate the types of comments and interpersonal dynamics that might arise.

Remote Generation of Ideas

With the advent of better communications technology and the Internet, it has become possible and often desirable for stakeholders to generate ideas remotely as part of a concept mapping process. Some of the advantages to this approach include the following:

- The ability to generate ideas among large stakeholder groups, often numbering in the hundreds, that would be unwieldy and difficult to manage within a live meeting format.

- No need for participants to travel.
- The ability for stakeholders to generate ideas in an environment where they are surrounded by their own resources and colleagues, thus increasing the depth of these contributions versus an off-site meeting.
- More time for participants to conceive and submit their ideas.
- Reduced effort in recording ideas, particularly when these ideas are submitted electronically.

There are some disadvantages to the remote model for generating idea statements:

- Less interactivity or exchange of ideas among the stakeholders themselves than there would be during a live process.
- A longer timeframe for this portion of the process, generally keeping a brainstorming mechanism available to participants for days or weeks versus hours.
- A greater chance for duplication of ideas during the brainstorming stage, leading to further effort in processing these statements.
- Unlike on-site brainstorming, which facilitates high levels of participation, remote brainstorming is generally subject to a much lower response rate. In general, we assume that a certain percentage of invited participants will not respond to a remote brainstorming request. The facilitator can mitigate many of the negative effects of technology both by assuring that the technology is easily accessible and easy to use and by establishing a comprehensive communications plan that engages participants throughout the life of the project.

Given the pros and cons of this approach, remote idea generation works best in an environment that involves large groups, geographically dispersed stakeholders, or both. It is also useful for situations in which it is advantageous to have a greater number of responses or a longer period of response time— for example, cases in which stakeholders wish to research issues or consult with colleagues as part of the idea generation process.

Remote idea generation activities generally take one of four forms:

- *Web-Based Input.* One of the most common forms of remote input is to invite participants to visit a Web page where they can enter their own idea statements in response to a focus prompt, usually via an electronic mail invitation. Figure 3.2 shows an example of a sample input screen for remote Web-based brainstorming, taken from the Concept Global program developed by Concept Systems.
- *Electronic Mail.* Participants can also submit statements directly via electronic mail to a specified address for processing.
- *Fax.* A fax number is provided for submitting statements via facsimile. This technique is useful for transmission of idea statements that are captured in hard-copy format.
- *Mail.* A mailing address is provided for submission of idea statements on paper.

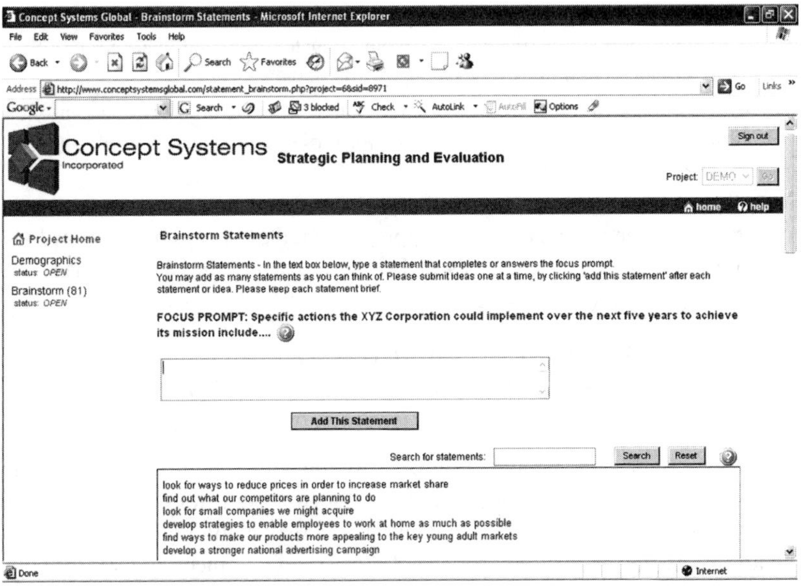

Figure 3.2 A Web Page Used for Brainstorming of Idea Statements by Remote Participants

SOURCE: Concept Global software, courtesy of Concept Systems, Inc., www.conceptsystems .com.

Steps in creating a successful remote idea generation session include the following:

- *Define Responsibilities.* Assign people to coordinate the remote brainstorming process, including the tasks outlined below.

- *Set Up Contact Information for Remote Brainstorming.* Create and "pilot test" a Web page for remote participant input and set up account information for each person accessing the results of this input. Where appropriate, also set up mail and fax addresses for paper input.

- *Identify Remote Participants.* Create a list of remote participants, including their e-mail addresses and other contact information.

- *Send Invitations and Background Information on the Project.* Draft an invitation with complete information for participants. Normally, this would be sent via electronic mail, with mail, fax, or telephone contact used where appropriate. For ease of use, consider having e-mail invitations include a clickable hyperlink with the address of the participant Web site.

- *Monitor Response Rates and Follow Up.* Keep track of people who respond to the invitation and participate in remote brainstorming, and plan to send follow-up reminders to those who have not yet participated.
- *Process the Responses.* Gather remote input from participants and consolidate them in a form that is easily accessed for further processing.

Most of these steps can be incorporated into the planning process outlined in Chapter 2 for the overall concept mapping effort; they should be integrated with other remote participant activities such as sorting and rating the statements.

INTRODUCE THE CONCEPT MAPPING
AND BRAINSTORMING PROCESS

This important step involves informing participants about the nature of the concept mapping process, as well as the specific brainstorming process they will participate in. This initial orientation and explanation of the process normally takes the form of a short agenda for an on-site meeting or instructions to remote participants. A chart similar to the process outline shown in Chapter 1 can be used to describe the steps in the process. Showing a typical final concept map from some other study would demonstrate to the group that their product is achievable.

The focus statement that was negotiated during the preparation step is the prompt for the brainstorming session. The concept mapping method generally applies the rules for brainstorming (Adams, 1979; Osborn, 1948): people are encouraged to generate many statements and are told that there should be no criticism or discussion regarding the legitimacy of statements generated during the session. Participants are encouraged to ask for clarification of any unfamiliar terms or jargon so everyone may understand what was intended by a given statement. Concept mapping brainstorming differs a little from traditional brainstorming, because it is not an "anything goes" approach to problem solving, but rather a very targeted exercise to elicit all possible issues, ideas, or knowledge in response to the focus prompt or statement. It is the task of the facilitator to help the participants apply that filter to their responses without discouraging input or participation.

Occasionally, some of the participants may hesitate to state their ideas because they fear—legitimately or not—that negative consequences may result. During the preparatory negotiations, the initiators may let the facilitator know, directly or subtly, that the conceptualization focus is the topic of considerable controversy or that the participants consist of subgroups that may be in conflict. The facilitator may then implement some process to allow for anonymous and confidential submission of ideas outside of the normal group brainstorming session. In one such study, the participants included both the staff of the organization and the members of the board. These groups had not worked together in the past, and the initiator warned us that there was some hostility between members of each group. Apparently, some staff members felt that the board did not have an appropriate assessment of its own role and interfered with staff's performance of responsibilities. Conversely, some board members felt that the staff was exceeding its appropriate role and taking the organization in an inappropriate direction. As facilitators, we decided that it would be necessary to allow participants to submit ideas that might be critical of the other group. At the brainstorming session, we explained that very often some people had difficulty or reluctance in expressing themselves in a public forum and that they could write some of their ideas on slips of paper and submit them outside of the group session. In this way, some very critical ideas were able to be entered without targeting any participant for the idea.

MANAGE THE BRAINSTORMING PROCESS

A brainstorming session involves much more than passively waiting for participants to share ideas—it requires active involvement and skills from the facilitator to keep discussions on track and ensure a smooth flow of ideas. The facilitation role is crucial in a brainstorming session: it represents a delicate balance between social and group pressures to conform with group norms and moments of silence when the group has apparently exhausted topic-related ideas. To manage an effective session, the facilitator must do the following:

- Keep the group on track, but at the same time not influence or distort its thinking.
- Point out when a brainstormed idea may be outside the scope of the brainstorming, while avoiding the role of conceptual gatekeeper.
- Decide when the session should be ended, but avoid ending it prematurely and risking the perception of exclusion.
- Manage the discussion itself, recognizing without bias whose turn it is to speak and preventing individuals from dominating the session.

The facilitator is responsible for managing any conflicts that might arise. For instance, participants may disagree about the wording of a particular statement. The facilitator must sense how to intervene in such cases. Sometimes the facilitator may suggest some compromise wording by combining suggestions within a single statement; at other times both wordings can be retained as separate statements. The facilitator must be in command of the discussion, but must stay as free as possible from determining the content. Keeping these responsibilities in mind, each facilitator can and should develop a unique approach to managing the brainstorming session.

The goal of a brainstorming session is to develop a set of items that represents the diversity of thought regarding the conceptual focus. Therefore, the facilitator should not allow the participants to become overly concerned with the nuances of any individual statement or idea, or whether redundancy exists between two statements. This is for two reasons. First, the focus on the language of a particular statement is sometimes a control device for someone in the group who desires attention to specific statements because of his or her position or expertise. Second, disputes about subtle distinctions of phrases are important, but they don't have to be resolved at this stage of the process. In fact, it is even desirable to allow a certain amount of redundancy among the statements. If two statements differ only slightly in wording and meaning, they should be close to each other on the final concept map. When the participants observe this, they are more likely to be convinced of the credibility of the whole process.

The facilitator should prepare for some likely situations that can arise during a brainstorming session. It helps to have some "stock" answers in mind for such issues. For instance, in many brainstorming sessions, a participant may suggest an idea that is questioned by another person. Questions might include: "What do you mean by that?" or "Why don't we phrase it this way . . . ?" or, even more aggressively, "What does that idea have to do with this problem?" The facilitator must consider several factors in deciding how to respond to this common situation. First, he or she would not want to disrupt the flow of the brainstorming session. If possible, it is best to resolve the issue and move on as quickly as possible. Second, the facilitator does not want to alienate any of the participants or encourage conflicts. Very often, the participants naturally fall into subgroups that are antithetical or have opposing interests (like board and staff). Third, the facilitator should diagnose what is happening very quickly. The preparation step should alert the facilitator to some of the existing intergroup and interpersonal conflicts. Sometimes it is apparent that a suggestion about rewording or rephrasing is readily acceptable to the participant who initially generated the statement. Even though the traditional rules of brainstorming maintain that there should be no criticism of brainstormed items, it may be more disruptive in some situations to cut off a readily acceptable suggested rewording than to remind the participants of the rules. If the facilitator is sensitive to what is happening in the session, it will often be apparent whether a quick, acceptable resolution is possible. Finally, the facilitator must be aware of the role of the brainstorming step within the broader context of the entire concept mapping process. When conflicts do arise, the facilitator can remind the participants that the purpose of the session is to generate lots of ideas, not to resolve disputes, and that even conflicting ideas can be entered.

IDEA SYNTHESIS: REDUCE AND EDIT
THE STATEMENT SET

The number of statements included in the process and their clarity to participants are key factors in the success of the subsequent concept mapping process. This means that, for many if not most brainstorming sessions, steps must be taken to reduce and edit the resulting set of ideas. Accomplishing this in a manner that preserves the overall integrity of the set of brainstormed ideas is a process we refer to as *idea synthesis*.

There are four main purposes of the idea synthesis process:

- To obtain a list of unique ideas, with only one idea represented in each statement
- To ensure that each statement is relevant to the focus of the project
- To reduce the statements to a manageable number for the stakeholders to sort and rate
- To edit statements for clarity and comprehension across the entire stakeholder group

The idea synthesis process is NOT intended to prioritize or remove specific ideas—this information will surface during the rating phase of the project. Rather, this is the time to ensure that stakeholders have a clear, understandable, relevant list of ideas that are not redundant.

Statement Synthesis

Although there is no limit to the number of statements that can be generated, large numbers of statements can impose serious practical constraints such as excessive time for data input, unnecessary redundancy of the content, and a loss of group energy. Our experience has led us to limit the number of statements to 100 or fewer. If the brainstorming session generates more than 100 statements—a common occurrence nowadays, particularly with large, remote brainstorming efforts—we then reduce the set by synthesizing common statements.

There are a number of approaches one can take for the statement synthesis process itself. The group as a whole or some subgroup can examine the set of statements for redundancies or ones that can be chosen to represent a set of others. In some instances, we have asked participants to examine a selected set of items to be sure that no key ideas were omitted. For instance, in one study (Linton, 1989a) the facilitator randomly selected 150 statements out of a larger set of 710 statements that were generated. In many contexts, a more formal analysis might be warranted, such as the various approaches of content analysis (Krippendorf, 2004). On several occasions we used a "keywords in context" form of content analysis on the items that were brainstormed. In most cases, however, some simple guidelines can be employed to reduce the statement set:

1. *Choose Keywords.* By highlighting keywords in the recorded ideas, it becomes easier to sort and evaluate potentially redundant ideas—particularly with the aid of a tool such as a spreadsheet, in which these keywords can be recorded in a separate column.

2. *Organize Ideas.* Group the ideas for reduction purposes on the basis of keywords, topics, or other conceptual areas.

3. *Choose Ideas.* Within a similar group of ideas, participants can form a consensus on which ideas to keep within a statement group. A binary (yes or no) "vote" or ranking value can also be recorded in a spreadsheet to facilitate the actual statement reduction process. This process can be done with a small group, such as a core group of stakeholders, who can vote on specific groups of statements using this ranking data.

4. *Edit for Clarity.* Participant ideas can be edited judiciously so that they are syntactically similar and express the original idea of the participant in a way that will be understood by more people.

5. *Split Compound Ideas.* It is perfectly acceptable to split a statement with two or more distinct ideas (such as "Create a tobacco quitline and a youth intervention program") into its component parts.

A process such as this will help produce a manageable number of statements, ideally within the guideline of 100 or fewer final statements. However, the idea synthesis process should ideally involve more than simply statement reduction—it should also ensure a clear and pertinent set of ideas for the sorting and rating process that follows.

Editing Considerations

Once a final set of statements has been generated, it is valuable for the group to examine them for editing considerations. Sometimes the wording of statements generated in a brainstorming session is awkward or technical jargon is not clear. In general, each statement should be consistent with what was called for in the brainstorming prompt and should be detailed enough so that every member of the group can understand the essential meaning of the statement. One simple approach is to read the brainstorming prompt immediately followed by each statement to assure that the statement grammatically completes the prompt appropriately. In editing, one should attempt to preserve the original meaning of the item as much as possible. In general, it is useful to keep the editing to a minimum. It should primarily involve correcting spelling or grammar mistakes. If extensive editing is required, it may be desirable to select a subgroup of participants to accomplish or approve this task, rather than to manage this with the entire participant group.

SOME ALTERNATIVES FOR GENERATING THE CONCEPTUAL DOMAIN

In most concept mapping processes, brainstorming is the method used to generate the conceptual domain. There are many advantages to brainstorming.

- People are familiar with it, because they are likely to have used brainstorming methods before.
- Brainstorming enables a group to generate a large set of ideas within a short period of time.
- On-site brainstorming generates ideas in a meeting or other public setting—all of the participants can hear each other's ideas as the session progresses. Thus, brainstorming has a synergistic effect—one person's idea often suggests things to other participants.
- Remote brainstorming engages the input of potentially large groups of people over a period of time, which encourages thoughtful and well-researched responses.

Despite the obvious advantages of brainstorming, it will not always be the method of choice. In this section, several other techniques are presented that demonstrate alternative ways to generate the conceptual domain, where the method used can be tailored to the specific setting.

Predetermined Statement Sets

In some concept mapping situations, the statement set will be dictated by the goals of the process. In one study, an organization consisting of 11 different departments wanted to determine whether the administrative structure could be streamlined or modified. We decided on concept mapping of the departments themselves to see how the participants perceived interdepartmental similarities. In this case, the set of statements consisted of the names of the 11 departments, and no formal generation process was needed. Similarly, if concept mapping is used as the foundation for evaluation, it may be desirable to use some predefined theoretical categories or scale items as the statement set. This was the case for Marquart (1989), who used a fixed number of categories defined from the research literature to map participant understanding of the issues involved in organizationally sponsored childcare; as well as the study conducted by Caracelli and Greene (1993), who used the 100 California Q-Sort personality items.

Text Abstraction and Keywords in Context

Most organizations and groups generate an enormous amount of text in the normal course of their work. A constant flow of reports, memos, field summaries, case records, minutes of meetings, and correspondence describes the ideas currently under consideration. In some contexts, this naturally occurring "text database" can be used as the basis for the generation of the set of ideas that are used for concept mapping. For instance, if the goal is to conduct long-term strategic planning for an organization, one might use a sample of interoffice memos and annual reports to generate all or part of the set of ideas. Similarly, when conducting qualitative research, abstracting ideas from field observers' notes might be the first step in the qualitative data analysis, in order to develop a concept map of the major themes in the data.

Text abstraction is any procedure used to select a set of ideas from some text documents. One common approach—called keywords in context (KWIC)—is a good example. The KWIC approach (Krippendorf, 2004; Stone et al., 1966) is one approach among many that uses content analysis to enable analysis of large text documents. The input consists of the text for a document or set of documents, and the output consists of an alphabetical list of all keywords within the context of their surrounding sentences. Figure 3.3 illustrates the output resulting from a KWIC application. Each keyword is listed alphabetically down the center of the page with as much of the preceding and following text displayed as possible on a single line. This enables the facilitator to review content and identify redundancies and unique statements.

There are other ways to abstract text from written documents. For instance, Dumont (1989) used the "documentary coding method" described by Wrightson (1976) to abstract statements from interview records. Whatever procedure is used, it is important that the rules for abstraction and the document sources be spelled out in detail so others might be able to judge the appropriateness of the procedure.

```
 . . .
315                    Jointly sponsor (w/   AAA )        conferences to raise community's awaren
355                           Partner with   AACPI        and state pain initiatives to develop
592   ealth systems on the resources available for   ACAP.
350       Outreach to church communities to encourage   acceptance              of palliative care.
 29   s for primary care staff & social workers on   access             to home health & hospice.
 36                        Assist in providing   access      to care (mental health, reimbursement,
 92   te a social service contact to help hospices   access      community services for indigent patie
190                               Enhance   access      to home care for the dying, allowing
269                               Improve   access      to care for all individuals, children
407    seling, education, health care resources and   access      linkage to end of life clients and ca
498                     Seriously ill people should have   access      to counseling and family support prio
506   s in libraries & health depts to help people   access          information, answers, & resources.
526   L care (reimbursement, eligibility, quality,   access).
544                     Support universal   access                  to quality EOL care.
574                     To have immediate   access      to referrals for pain management, hos
622   administered by the aging network to ensure   access                      to hospice care.
398                               Provide   accessible       and usable resources to guide pat
399                               provide   accurate       info & refer to other agencies who
361    ociation for Death Education and Counseling   (ACED).
 81   olunteers to assist w/ practical tasks or to   act                     as companions.
252   state pass the Uniform Healthcare Decisions   Act .
394   on of the Uniform Healthcare Decision-Making   Act .
548   equirement of the Patient Self-Determination   Act .
 . . .
```

Figure 3.3   Keyword in Context (KWIC) Sample Output

SUMMARY

The generation step is usually the first contact that the entire participant group has with the concept mapping process. It sets the tone for subsequent steps and establishes the credibility of both the facilitator and of the process itself. On-site or remote brainstorming is the usual method employed for generating statements, although in certain situations the statement set may be predefined or the statements may be abstracted from text documents or interviews. Once defined, the statement set is considered the conceptual domain for the process; it is the basis of the structuring step described in the next chapter.

EXERCISES

For this set of exercises, you may follow one of two options. If you performed the exercises in the previous chapter, you may use the goals and focus statement from them as the basis for this exercise. If you did not, or if you wish to try a different concept mapping task, select some new topic that might constitute the focus for these exercises. A good way to do this might be to find a newspaper or magazine article that addresses some topic of interest (e.g., public school education, drug-related criminal activity, defense department spending). Define a suitable focus statement for this problem area.

1. Plan a short brainstorming session for the concept mapping problem. Use the checklist provided in Table 3.1 to help guide the planning. Do a "dry run" of the brainstorming with a few friends or classmates. Limit the number of statements to 50 or fewer. Afterward, discuss with others:
   a. How smoothly did the session go? Were there certain people who dominated the session and seemed to control the content? Were there difficulties or disputes regarding the wording of statements? How did you address these issues?
   b. How would you assess the quality of the set of statements? Is the set comprehensive or are there major issues you feel were left out?
   c. What changes, if any, would you make to the checklist in Table 3.1?

2. Obtain a short written piece about the issue being studied. If you are using the focus from the exercises in the previous chapter, you may want to write a short hypothetical position paper on the issue or create an imaginary memo on the topic. If you are using a newspaper or magazine article for the focus, then you're all set.

3. For a *short* passage in the written piece (only one or two paragraphs), manually conduct a KWIC analysis following these steps.
   a. Read through the passage and write down all trivial or nonkey terms (e.g., the, it). This list will constitute your exception dictionary.
   b. On a double-spaced copy of the passage, number all of the remaining keywords. Write each of these words on a separate index card along with its number.
   c. Put the set of index cards into alphabetical order.
   d. On wide paper, write the alphabetized key words in a column down the middle of the page. Use the key word index number to locate the word in the passage. For each key word, write as much of the proceeding and following text as will fit on a single line.

e. Examine the KWIC listing you have constructed. Are there any keywords that occurred more than once? Are you able to see any general themes that are implied by these clusterings of keywords? How might you use this listing to construct a small set of statements that describes the passage well?

f. Imagine that instead of doing this by hand, you were able to submit a larger text passage to a KWIC computer program. How would the listing help you to devise a set of statements suitable for concept mapping?

4. Using a much larger passage of text (perhaps the entire article or memo), construct your own procedure for abstracting a meaningful set of statements for concept mapping. Write down the rules you use to abstract statements from the text. Give the passage and the written rules to a friend or classmate, and have them also abstract statements from the text. Discuss the following:

a. Examining the statements you derived, do they adequately represent the content of the passage?

b. How does your set compare with the set derived by the other person?

c. How does your set compare with the brainstormed statements obtained in Exercise 1 above?

d. What do you think the implications of these alternative methods for generating statements would be for the final concept mapping product?

4

Structuring the Statements

To someone who has thought much, every new idea he hears or reads, immediately appears as a chain.

—Friedrich Nietzsche

At this point in the process, before structuring begins, the following have been created:

- A specific focus to accomplish the desired outcome of the study
- A group of participants who may be representative of specific relevant populations, or individuals who have the required knowledge to inform the study
- A list of around 100 comments, observations, or ideas that are directly related to the purpose of the study

Structuring builds on these elements and involves two separate but equally important conceptual tasks. First, participants provide their perceptions of the similarities between statements. Second, in most concept mapping projects, they also rate each statement on some dimension by answering the rating focus question for each idea. These two tasks constitute the structuring of the conceptual domain. In addition, in order to enable subgroup analyses of this structuring information, participants also contribute basic demographic or organizational information.

This chapter describes how to manage the structuring tasks in a concept mapping project. At the end of the chapter, we will also present several alternative methods for structuring the data. Figure 4.1 presents an overview flowchart of the steps involved in the structuring process.

This process includes the following core steps:

- *Plan the Structuring Activity.* Arranging facilities, logistics, and materials for sorting and rating activities
- *Introduction and Agendas.* Providing a project update and overview of session activities to participating stakeholders
- *Sort Statements.* Facilitating the sorting of statements into individual groupings by participants, and preserving these results for later coding and analysis
- *Rate Statements.* Facilitating the rating of each statement by participants

Structuring

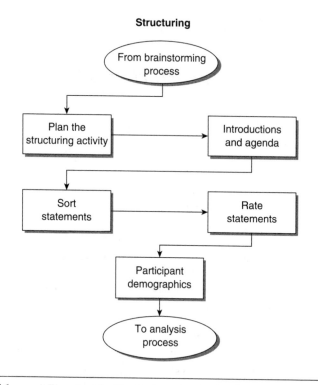

Figure 4.1   A Flowchart for Conducting a Structuring Session

- *Participant Demographics or Organizational Characteristics.* Tracking participant information such as organizational affiliation, type of stakeholder, or geographic region for later use in pattern matching analysis or comparing concept
  mapping results

The result of this process is the raw data needed to execute a concept mapping
analysis and generate concept maps, pattern matching, and go-zone displays of
results. As a result, careful attention at this phase of the process is perhaps the
most important aspect of creating high-value results for involved stakeholders.

Depending on the needs of the project, the facilitator will help the initiator
choose between two possible approaches for structuring the statements:

- Hold on-site meetings in which stakeholders sort and/or rate the statements. This
  approach is best suited to specific organizations or groups of stakeholders within
  a single geographic location, as well as event-based meetings such as a conference or committee meeting.

- Invite people to sort and rate statements, using a Web-based interface or other technology-supported method, in much the same manner as the initial brainstorming step. This approach works best with large or geographically distributed groups of stakeholders.

First, we will look at issues in managing an on-site structuring session, and then examine the specifics of managing a remote structuring effort.

PLAN THE STRUCTURING ACTIVITY

The basic ingredients for planning a successful structuring session are communication, method selection, materials development, site preparation, and the meeting plan. Table 4.1 provides a simple checklist to help prepare for the structuring session.

As always, the facilitator is responsible for assuring that the participants are aware of the logistics (location, time, etc.) and agenda of the session. Communication in advance of the session is usually drafted and coordinated with the client or initiator to make sure that the tone, content, and instructions are clear and appropriate for the audience.

At the initial negotiations for the concept mapping process, the facilitator and initiators should agree about which methods they will use to obtain the sorting and rating information. Usually, this is accomplished with card sorting and a rating questionnaire (as previously described), but several alternatives, which we discuss at the end of the chapter, are also available.

All of the relevant materials, including an agenda, statement decks, rating questionnaires, demographics forms, and overall instructions, should be ready well in advance of the meeting. To help make the sorting task more useful, the facilitator will randomize the statements before creating the statement sets, so that "like" ideas generated during the brainstorming session are no longer necessarily near each other in the packet of ideas. If the facilitator is responsible for producing the materials, he or she may provide them at the meeting. If the initiator or client group is to provide them, the facilitator will confirm their availability before the meeting and have backup masters, at least, of all needed materials.

The setting should be checked to make sure that it is appropriate and comfortable for the participants. If the participants are going to sort cards, it is especially important to ensure that there is enough table space for them to work comfortably because that activity requires square footage per person. Supplies like pencils, rubber bands, and so on should be on hand, and a photocopier should be nearby in the event of emergencies.

Table 4.1
A Checklist for Preparing for the On-Site Structuring Session

Task	Person Assigned	Completion Date
Advance Notice		
Send invitation or announcement to all participants		
Send follow-up reminder (by e-mail, phone, or mail)		
Send short (1 page) project update to participants		
Materials		
Session agenda packet with participant instructions		
Card decks of randomly ordered statements (following statement reduction where appropriate)		
Sort recording sheet		
Rating questionnaire		
Demographics questionnaire		
Setup		
Comfortable seating where all can see and participate		
Adequate lighting and sound		
Card sorting instructions posted and clearly visible		
Sufficient table space for card sorting		
Rating focus statement posted and clearly visible		
Dry Run		
Timed work plan for the session, with assigned speakers and content		
"Pilot-testing" of rating prompt		

The facilitator will develop a meeting plan—an outline of the sequence of steps for the session and of what will be said at each step. The agenda will serve as the outline for the meeting plan, and the initiator (or meeting host if different from the initiator) and the facilitator will develop the sequence of activities and area of responsibility each might have for the meeting's success.

INTRODUCTION AND AGENDAS

The facilitator and initiator will have agreed in advance about the best way to open the session; on occasion, the initiator welcomes participants, reintroduces the facilitator, and sets the tone and expected outcomes for the session. He or she may decide instead simply to turn it over to the facilitator to lay the groundwork. As with virtually all elements of a concept mapping process, it all depends on the need, the audience, and the desired outcome for that activity. The facilitator is usually responsible for presenting the agenda and fielding any questions the group may have. Time management is very important in all sessions with participants; respect for the value of their time is balanced with the need to ensure understanding of what has gone on before and what will take place in the present, as well as time to ask questions. The session may include, if necessary, a brief orientation for the participants about the concept mapping process and the current task.

SORT STATEMENTS

At this stage of the process, the participants are ready to sort the statements into groupings. The facilitator provides instructions for this sorting process, oversees the execution of it, and ensures that the results of the sorting are recorded.

Sorting things into piles of similar items is a most common human activity; it helps to organize complexity in one's context. The grouping, or sorting, of disparate statements or ideas into piles helps identify a stakeholder's view of the interrelationships of the ideas. In this methodology, we refer to this as a "sorting" task, because we ask the participants to sort the cards into piles or groups, and because that terminology is consistent with the research literature (see Block [1961] on Q-sort, Rosenberg & Kim [1975], on unstructured card sorting, Weller & Romney [1988] on the pile sort, and Cataldo [1970] or

Coxon [1999] on sorting generally). Over the course of the last 18 years or so, the term has become widely accepted and understood as meaning the arrangement of items into sets of like ideas, rather than an ordering or ranking of statements for relative value.

Instructions for Statement Card Sorting and Results Recording

The facilitator might use the introduction to this activity to move into the present and draw the group's attention to the next logical task: the sorting and recording. Before the statement decks are handed out, the facilitator uses the written instructions he or she has provided as a tool to make sure that the participants understand the instructions, allotting time for questions and clarification. The card decks are then distributed and the participants are given time to do the sorting. The amount of time it takes to do the sorting varies considerably from person to person. With approximately 100 statements, participants may require anywhere from 20 to 50 minutes (or more, on occasion) to group the statements. A short break outside the meeting room should be allowed for those who finish ahead so that others won't be distracted.

For the sorting task, each of the generated statements and its unique statement identification number are printed on a separate card, and each participant receives the complete set of cards. The facilitator then instructs each person to sort, or group, the cards into piles "in a way that makes sense to you." Three major restrictions are applied here:

- All statements cannot be put into a single pile.
- All statements cannot be put into their own separate piles (although *some* statements may be grouped by themselves).
- Each statement can be placed in only one pile (i.e., a statement can't be placed in two piles at the same time).

The first two restrictions are included because if a person puts all items into one pile, or every one into its own, they are supplying no information about the *interrelationships* among the statements. The last restriction is like a forced-choice response format on a questionnaire—although a statement may sensibly be grouped in more than one pile, the participant is forced to decide where it is "best" located. Excepting these conditions, people may group the cards in any way that makes sense to them. Often the participants perceive that there may be several different ways to group the cards, all of which make sense. To address this, we have either instructed participants to select the "most sensible" arrangement or, in some studies, had each participant sort the cards several times.

Record Statement Sorting Results

Each participant has a unique set of data as the result of his or her sort activity. Some may have many groups of ideas that represent unique concepts for the participant, and others may have sorted ideas into only four or five groups. After completing that step, each participant records the results of his or her work on a sort recording sheet, which is provided with the statement cards (see Figure 4.2) The form can be very simple, and participants are instructed to review the contents of each grouping, pile by pile, and come up with a "placeholder" name for that grouping. The participant writes the name of the first group he or she is considering, then lists the statements in that group *by identifying number*, with commas or slash separators between each unique identifying number. The participant then goes on to the next pile and conducts the same process, until all groupings are represented by the title and a line of numbers that represent the related statements. This technique has the advantage of requiring less work on the part of the facilitators in data entry of results, although legibility and completeness are occasional problems.

If for some reason it is impossible to have the participants record their sorting results, the facilitator may collect the raw data, i.e., the statement cards kept separated into the groupings that the participant made. Perhaps the simplest way to keep the piles separate is to place rubber bands around the card decks after cross-laying the card piles. This can be difficult, so care must be taken. In some projects, we have labeled the decks with the name of the participant or an ID number, so that we might later compute subgroup maps. If no subgroup analyses are anticipated, no identification is necessary.

RATE STATEMENTS

For the next step of the process, the participants normally rate the statements on the basis of the specified rating focus prompt. This step is not necessary for the generation of the basic point and cluster concept maps—however, these rating values are, of course, a required and integral part of rating-based displays such as pattern matches and go-zones. The facilitator will once again provide instructions for this process, oversee the execution of it, and ensure that its results are recorded.

SORT RECORDING SHEET

NOTE: Return this sheet in the envelope provided.

NAME: _____

This sheet is to be used for **Task 1, Step 2—Recording the Results.**
Specific directions for recording your sorts are included in the Instructions
for Task 1—Sorting and Recording. **Remember that you do not have to
have as many piles as there are boxes on this Sheet. The space is
provided to allow for variability among participants in the way they
group the items. The first box (Example Stack) is filled out to serve
as a guide for you.**

Example Stack Title or Main Topic: Program Management
Record here the identifying number of each item in this stack, separating the
ID numbers with commas.

1, 4, 29, 43, 12

Stack Title or Main Topic: _____
Record here the identifying number of each item in this stack, separating the
ID numbers with commas.

Stack Title or Main Topic: _____
Record here the identifying number of each item in this stack, separating the
ID numbers with commas.

Figure 4.2   Excerpt of a Sort Recording Sheet for Participant Statement Sorting

Rating Instructions and the Rating of Statements

Once the cards have been sorted, collected, and recorded, the rating instructions can be given. Each participant receives a rating sheet upon which he or she will rate each of the statements, according to the instruction provided by the rating focus described in Chapter 2. The rating focus statement and rating scale should be clearly visible at all times. If possible, these can be included in the written instructions at the top of the rating questionnaire. Figure 4.3 shows a sample rating sheet.

There is a sound theoretical reason for conducting the sorting of items *before* assigning the ratings. The sorting task encourages the participants to

---

RATING SHEET
MENTAL HEALTH PLANNING PROJECT

Focus Prompt
Generate statements which describe services which our agency does or might provide.

Rate each statement on a 1 to 5 scale where 1 = Relatively Unimportant; 2 = Somewhat Important; 3 = Moderately Important; 4 = Very Important; 5 = Extremely Important

					#	Statement
1	2	3	4	5	(1)	Marriage counseling
1	2	3	4	5	(2)	Evaluation services—testing for courts, Dept. of Human Services, school systems
1	2	3	4	5	(3)	Hypnosis/relaxation
1	2	3	4	5	(4)	Sexual abuse services
1	2	3	4	5	(5)	Prevention/education workshops for community
1	2	3	4	5	(6)	Crisis treatment
1	2	3	4	5	(7)	Behavioral medicine—techniques to treat pain, eating disorders, phobias
1	2	3	4	5	(8)	Employee assistance programs
1	2	3	4	5	(9)	Outpatient services for the elderly
1	2	3	4	5	(10)	Outpatient services for the divorced
1	2	3	4	5	(11)	Outpatient services for offenders

Figure 4.3   Excerpt of a Rating Sheet for Participant Statement Rating

attend to the semantic similarities between statements, regardless of how each participant might feel about the importance or priority of each statement. The rating task explicitly addresses each participant's perception of an item's importance or other relevant value qualifier. These are generally more emotionally charged units of judgment that are usually subject to a wider range of views. If the rating task is done first, it is likely that it will influence how the participants sort the cards, because they will already have formed a mental set that addresses the rating focus. In this case, they would be likely to sort their top-priority items together, their low-priority items together, and so on, negating semantically meaningful similarities among the items.

The rating is usually a Likert-type response scale (e.g., ratings between 1 and 5 or between 1 and 7), which indicates some quantity to be associated with each statement. This can take the form of subjective rating values such as importance, feasibility, priority, effort, or some other expected outcome. They also can take the form of any other kind of value associated with each statement, such as its estimated cost. More than one rating can be conducted in a single concept mapping project, and that is often desirable. If the goal of the mapping is to provide a basis for operational planning, the participants might be asked to rate each statement (i.e., action or activity) for how much priority it should be given *and* for the level of resources it will require.

There is a tendency for participants to fall into a "response set" when performing ratings. For instance, if a priority rating is requested, many persons will resist assigning low priorities for a statement. After all, if a statement was brainstormed, it must have *some* priority. Although this may be true in an absolute sense, it is usually better to encourage the participants to make a *relative* judgment instead. They might be encouraged to do this with an instruction like the following:

> Before doing your ratings, quickly scan the entire list of statements to try to get an idea of which ones are of highest and lowest priority within the set. Then, when you rate the statements, try to use the *full range* of rating values (e.g., 1 to 5).

This kind of instruction encourages participants to do a better job of determining the *relative* values of the statements.

PARTICIPANT DEMOGRAPHICS

In addition to collecting sorting and rating information, most concept mapping studies collect specified demographic or organizational information from participants, to allow for subsequent analysis of results based on these demographic criteria. For example, this demographic information can be used to analyze how clusters of ideas are rated by managers compared to staff members, or by service providers compared to consumers. Examples of demographic data include the following:

- Type of organization
- Tenure within current organization
- Level of responsibility (manager, staff, board member, etc.)
- Geographic location
- Degree of specialization

IMPORTANCE RATING FORM DEMOGRAPHICS

**NOTE: Before you can complete the ratings, please
answer the following questions.**

NAME: _____

1. What participant category best describes your current position?

    _____ Public health agency

    _____ Private mental health

    _____ Community/advocacy group

    _____ Other

2. How long have you been in your current position?

    _____ years _____ months

Figure 4.4   Sample Participant Demographics Form

Figure 4.4 shows a sample sheet for collecting demographic data.

Because these data are inherently tied in with rating results for analysis purposes, they are normally collected at the same time as the rating data, generally as a sheet attached to the rating questionnaire.[1]

To avoid privacy concerns, participants should be reassured, both verbally and on the demographic information form itself, that their responses to these demographic questions will be not be used to identify them personally. During the analysis phase, this information will be used to compute results, such as cluster rating maps and pattern matching, where ratings can be compared between specific demographic subgroups identified on the questionnaire.

REMOTE STRUCTURING

Just as the participants can contribute to brainstorming remotely, as discussed in the previous chapter, participants can also sort and rate statements remotely using a communications or technology tool. Many situations can make an on-site process unfeasible, such as large groups whose members are geographically dispersed, or situations in which budgets, travel issues, or conflicting schedules create difficulties. Using technology (like an Internet program or e-mail) or independent participant communication (like fax or phone) can diminish this problem.

Sorting and rating activities are particularly well suited to remote implementation, because they are inherently solitary activities—participants sort and rate according to their own views and opinions of the aggregated set of ideas, so, strictly speaking, interaction with others is not necessary. But the same concerns about response rates exist here as they do for remote brainstorming. A remote structuring activity requires, in many cases, even more careful planning and participant follow-up than on-site activities. The time allotted for sorting and rating is often weeks rather than hours or days, to enable remote participants to complete the tasks when they can. The initiators and the facilitator should also have realistic expectations that not all participants will respond to the degree they would to an on-site meeting.

Strategies for remote structuring activities can include any of the following:

- *Web-Based Input.* Participants visit a Web page specifically designed to facilitate sorting and rating of the statement set and submit their results electronically together with participant demographic information. Figures 4.5 and 4.6 show examples of sample input screens for remote Web-based sorting and rating, taken from the Concept Global program.
- *Electronic Mail.* Participants can submit sorting, rating, and demographic results directly via electronic mail to a specified address using an electronic document format similar to that shown for the paper documents above.
- *Fax.* Participants can submit hardcopies of structuring forms via facsimile to a designated fax number.
- *Mail.* Participants can submit structuring forms on paper to a designated mailing address.

Because fax, e-mail, and mail participation basically applies the same process as on-site structuring—e.g., paper-based forms that are then forwarded to the facilitator—we concentrate here on Internet-based approaches to structuring.

The logistics for remote structuring sessions are very similar to the process described in Chapter 3 for remote brainstorming, including determining project responsibilities, defining the timeframe and communications infrastructure, inviting and tracking participants, following up with participants who have not responded, and gathering the results. At the conclusion of the process, results can once again be gathered and processed in much the same manner as a live structuring session. Only Web-based input enables the facilitator to import the data directly from the input collection point into a software program for analysis. The others require the same level of data input as the on-site data.

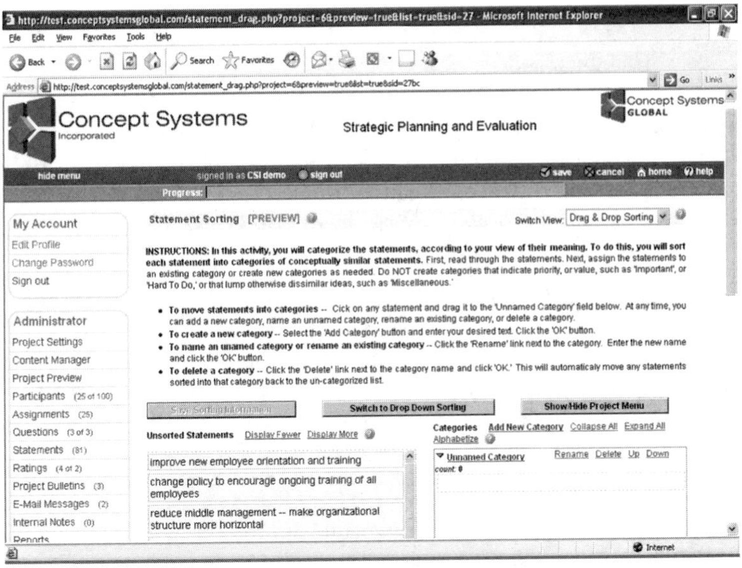

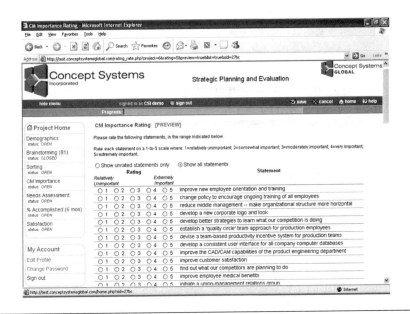

Figure 4.5   Web-Based Statement Sorting Form

Figure 4.6   Web-Based Statement Rating Form

ALTERNATIVE METHODS FOR STRUCTURING

As mentioned earlier, the typical way to structure the statements is to use an unstructured card sorting procedure. Participants easily understand the process, and it takes little time to group a large number of statements. There are, of course, other ways to structure the conceptual domain (Coxon, 1999; Trochim & Linton, 1986; Weller & Romney, 1988).

Variations on Card Sorting

The unstructured sorting method described above is the normative and fundamental approach typically used in concept mapping, but there are other variations documented in the literature, several of which we describe briefly.

Constrained Sorting

One option is to instruct participants to sort the cards into a fixed number of piles. Constrained sorting is usually done to counteract the tendencies of some participants to "lump" (use relatively few piles) and some to "split" (use relatively many piles). But, in comparisons of the constrained and unconstrained sorting procedures, there does not appear to be evidence that any great difference results (Burton, 1975).

Open-Choice Sorting

A second variation is to allow participants to group any single statement simultaneously into two or more piles. In this case, the data would be coded as described earlier, with statements in multiple piles being treated as though they were in each pile (Stefflre, Reich, & McClaran-Stefflre, 1971).

Tree Sorting

Some variations of the tree sort are useful for concept mapping (Weller & Romney, 1988). In a top-down sort, participants begin by dividing the statement cards into two piles. They then divide these two piles into two more, yielding four piles. This continues until each pile contains only one or two statements. In a bottom-up sort, participants begin by combining the two statements that are most similar into a pile. At each successive stage, they combine either two statements, a statement and a current pile, or two piles, until all statements are grouped together (Fillenbaum & Rappaport, 1971). These methods are appropriate only if it is reasonable to assume that a hierarchical structure is appropriate for the concepts at hand. Furthermore, the top-down approach does not yield data that can be easily aggregated into a single group similarity matrix. In this case, one would have to construct a similarity matrix for each participant and use an individual difference scaling (INDSCAL) model (Davison, 1983; Kruskal & Wish, 1978) for multidimensional scaling across individuals.

The Method of Triads

In the triadic method (Weller & Romney, 1988), all statements are grouped into all possible combinations of three. The participant is asked to indicate which of the three is most different from the others. The data are coded much the same way as in the sorting method described earlier. For each triad of statements (i.e., set of three), the pair not judged to be different is considered similar and a 1 is coded for that pair in the similarity matrix. Here, however, because each pair will turn up in more than one triad, the values in each (pairwise) cell are summed to yield the similarity for that pair. The method of triads is not feasible when the number of statements is large, so its use in concept mapping is limited.

Ranking and Rating for Similarity

Both of these approaches could be used for concept mapping by requiring the participants to either rank or rate the statements with respect to their similarity to some overarching concept or concepts. The facilitator must clearly define the rating described here as completely different from other ratings, such as for priority or importance, as described earlier. Here, ratings are judged solely to estimate the degree of similarity between statements, not their value with respect to some judgment dimension. In general, if either of these methods is used, multiple rankings or ratings would be desired, each with respect to a different concept. The results would then be aggregated within and then across participants. For instance, if each statement is rated on a 1–5 scale with respect to how similar it is to some target concept, the results would be coded into an $N \times N$ similarity matrix by coding items that have the same rating as being most similar, those with rating values one apart being coded as next most similar, and so on. For a 1–5 rating scale, the similarity matrix would have values ranging from 0 to 4 for each rating for each participant. Ranked data would be coded in a similar way—items that are close in rank would be considered more similar, and the similarity value for any pair would be the absolute value of the difference between their ranks. In both of these approaches, the major problem is in deciding how many rankings or ratings should be done, and what concepts should be used as the focus. However, the potential value of these alternatives is in their capability for yielding data to produce both individual and group concept maps, so ranking and rating methods should be considered when these are desired.

Outlining

An outline is a structure that implies similarities between entries, and could potentially be used for the structuring step. Participants could be given a set of statements and asked to organize them into an outline form with headings and subheadings. To code the outline into a similarity matrix, the facilitator presents some rules. In general, the rules maintain that all items under one subheading are coded as more similar than items under a different subheading. In a preliminary investigation of this approach (Cooksy, 1989), several different sets of rules or algorithms were examined, and some were found to be better than others. The major difficulty involves considering whether the ordering of headings and subheadings implies anything about similarity. For instance, for all headings at the same level of indentation, should two headings that are closer to each other be judged as more similar than headings that are farther apart? The potentially exciting aspect of outlining is that we might be able to automate the coding of outlines into a similarity matrix, and consequently would be able to compute an individual's concept map directly from the outline. Given the plethora of computerized outlining programs available, this would make it possible to move automatically from the hierarchical outline to a relational map. This would yield individual concept maps that then would require aggregation to create a multiparticipant conceptual framework. More work needs to be done along these lines (Cooksy, 1989) before we can be confident in the sensibility of any algorithms for outlining.

None of the sorting approaches provides enough information to enable one to compute maps for a single participant. If this is desired, and sorting procedures are used, each participant needs to group the cards multiple times. Dumont (1989) found that maps could be computed for participants who grouped the cards at least five times. For fewer sorts, the multidimensional scaling algorithm was sometimes incalculable. If individual maps are desired and multiple groupings are not feasible, another approach such as tree sorting (described earlier) might be used.

SUMMARY

The structuring process involves the collection of similarity and rating data about the set of statements, along with participant demographic information, employing either an on-site meeting or a remote process that is generally conducted on-line. Typically, we use an unstructured card sorting of the statements to obtain information about their similarities and a rating of importance, priority, or other relevant dimensions for the rating information. There are also many alternative methods for obtaining the similarity information (including constrained sorting, tree sorting, ranking, rating, and outlining), some of which provide data that enable both individual and group concept mapping.

NOTE

1. Based on experience, demographic information is generally used only in connection with rating data and not concept maps themselves because group differences in how similarity among items is perceived is often of less interest than differences in ratings. The implication of this in practice is that if we intend to combine all sorts in computing the map, it is not necessary, except for descriptive purposes, to collect demographics on participants who only sort. Similarly, in designs where different groups sort and rate, this may mean that only raters are given the demographics.

EXERCISES

In these exercises, you should use one of the sets of statements that you generated in the exercises in the previous chapter, or you should generate a new set before proceeding. The purpose of these exercises is to acquaint you with several methods for structuring the set of statements and with appropriate coding procedures.

1. Let's begin by doing the traditional unstructured sorting of the set of statements. Write each statement onto a separate card or slip of paper and number them in the order they were generated. Now, take the set of statements and group the statements into piles in a way that makes sense to you. Remember that you are sorting similar items into the same pile.

2. Now, have several of your friends pile the set of items. For each of them, record their piling results. Discuss the following:
   a. How did you feel when you piled the statements? Did you have trouble at times deciding which pile a statement should go in? How did you resolve the difficulty and make a decision?
   b. How similar were the groupings that different people did? Which pairs of items were put together by the most people? Do these seem to be the most similar pairs in the set of statements?
   c. Did different people experience similar difficulties in placing certain statements? Did they resolve these in the same ways? How are these decisions related to the conceptual meanings of these statements?
   d. Were there any difficulties in managing the sorting task? Did participants readily understand the instructions? How long did the process take for different participants? How would you improve the process in the future?

3. Try one or more of the following variations on the basic sorting procedure to become familiar with how they feel:
   a. The unstructured sorting procedure with a fixed number of piles. You might want to try two groupings—one into relatively few piles, and one into many piles.
   b. The unstructured sorting procedure allowing any statement to be in more than one pile at a time.
   c. The top-down sort, in which you first divide all of the statements into two piles. Now divide each of the piles into two more. Repeat this process until there are only two or three statements in each pile.

d. The bottom-up sort, which is just the opposite. First, pick the two statements that are most similar and place them together in a pile. Next, decide on the next highest similarity—it could be between two entirely new statements or between a statement and the existing cluster. Continue this process—at each stage combining either two statements, a statement and an existing pile, or two piles—until you have all of the statements into two or three piles.

e. For any of the variations above, what are their advantages and disadvantages over the traditional unstructured sorting method? Which of them take longer than others? Does the sorting task take longer? Can you think of any ways to streamline any of these methods to make them more efficient?

5

Concept Mapping Analysis

One picture is worth a thousand words.

—Fred R. Barnard

The heart of the concept mapping process is the sequence of analysis and mapping of the information produced in the structuring step: the data from each participant's sorting and rating of the brainstormed statements. The analysis begins with the data generated in the structuring step and ends with a set of materials (maps and statement listings, pattern matches, go-zones, and other reports) to be used as the basis of the interpretation session. Figure 5.1 is an overview of the steps involved in constructing the maps and preparing the results for the interpretation session.

After the data are entered, the analyst performs three steps in the core analysis to compute maps for the conceptual domain:

1. *Create similarity matrix* from sort data. The similarity matrix is a square symmetric matrix that shows the number of participants who sorted each pair of statements together in accomplishing their sorts.
2. *Multidimensional scaling (MDS)* of similarity matrix, to locate each statement as a separate point on a two-dimensional (X, Y) map (i.e., the point map).
3. *Hierarchical cluster analysis* of the multidimensional scaling (X, Y) coordinates to partition the points (statements) on this map into groups.

This core concept mapping analysis is typically completed once for each mapping project, although in a technology-assisted process, the analyst can produce results as often as needed. It is important to note that the analysis uses only the sorting data from the structuring step and produces the map (i.e., array of statements or points), and suggested cluster results, upon which all other analyses are conducted. Ratings data, which are used in ratings maps, pattern matches, and go-zones, are analyzed at the point when such results are called for. These ratings analyses use simple averaging or totaling of ratings data. Depending on the needs of the project, ratings results can be created at any time after the creation of the core map analysis.

The results of the core analysis require additional preparation in advance of the interpretation session that follows, as indicated in the box at the bottom of Figure 5.1. The additional steps in preparation for interpretation are as follows:

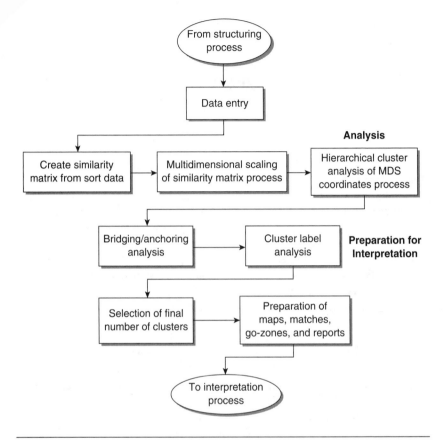

Figure 5.1   Flowchart of the Analysis Process

- *Bridging/anchoring analysis* to identify which statements and clusters are "anchors" in any specific area of the maps and which ones are "bridging" across areas of the map

- *Cluster label analysis* to identify labels from individual sorts that are the best prospective candidates for cluster labels on the map

- *Selection of the final number of clusters* from the results of the hierarchical cluster analysis

- *Preparation of materials* for the interpretation session including the maps, pattern matches, go-zones, and reports

All of these steps serve two purposes: to ensure that the analyst fully understands the map and the relationship of the information within it to the issue at hand, and to enable preparation of material that is specifically responsive to the interpretation audience and the purpose of the project. The bridging/anchoring and cluster label analyses are particularly useful to the analyst as background, and the selection of the final number of clusters is a critical decision that has implications for all subsequent cluster-level results.

Practically speaking, it is impossible to conduct these analyses manually. Even for very small group data or projects, multidimensional scaling and cluster analysis—fairly sophisticated multivariate analyses—require the use of computer programs for processing. The analyst has several options for computer software for conducting the concept mapping analyses. The Concept System program (Concept Systems Incorporated, 2005) was developed explicitly to accomplish the sequence of analyses used in concept mapping and can do all of the analyses described here. General-purpose statistical programs can also be used. Both SPSS (SPSS Inc., 2005) and SAS (SAS Institute, 2005) have routines that can accomplish multidimensional scaling and hierarchical cluster analysis. Beyond that, there are numerous multidimensional scaling routines available on the Web that will require some level of programming skill or advanced statistical knowledge to implement.

Because this volume is not a text on multivariate analysis, the interested reader is encouraged to consult the key literature on the creation of the similarity matrix (Coxon, 1999; Rosenberg & Kim, 1975; Weller & Romney, 1988), multidimensional scaling (Davison, 1983; Kruskal & Wish, 1978; Shepard, Romney, & Nerlove, 1972), and hierarchical cluster analysis (Anderberg, 1973; Everitt, 1980) or general texts on multivariate methods (Hair, Tatham, Anderson, & Black, 1998).

In this chapter, we describe these analyses in nontechnical terms and show how they are used within a concept mapping process. We describe each analysis step and show how the concept maps and related displays are constructed. The following sections look at each of these steps in more detail.

DATA ENTRY

The first step, of course, is to enter the data into the computer for analysis. There are a variety of ways to structure the sort data for aggregation in the data analysis. Perhaps the simplest is to create a matrix in which the rows correspond to the number of sorters and the columns to the number of statements. The value for each cell is the sort pile number the statement is in for that sorter. The next section describes how these data are aggregated.

The rating data are typically coded into a rectangular data matrix, in which each row or line is an individual participant and each column is a statement. The cells are the rating values for each person (row) for each statement (column). If multiple ratings are done in a project, a separate matrix will be needed for each statement. The average values for each statement can then be calculated across participants simply by obtaining summary statistics for each column.

Demographic data can be stored in a table in which there is a row for each participant and a column for each variable.

Depending on the schedule of the project, data input sometimes must occur immediately. We use concept mapping software (Concept Systems Incorporated, 2005) to enable fast turnaround for data input and analysis, but the time required for input of data collected manually should not be underestimated. Factors to consider include the number of statements, number of participants, and number of ratings collected. If we consider an average data unit for each participant to be a sort of 100 statements and one rating run of 100 statements, the facilitator should plan for between three and seven minutes per participant for data input.

ANALYSIS

Create Similarity Matrix

At the end of data collection (Chapter 4), the analyst has sort information from each key stakeholder participant that describes how they perceive the relationships between statements. When the sort recording forms have been collected, the results are combined across people to estimate the similarity among statements across the participants. This is accomplished in two steps, as illustrated in Figure 5.2.

First, the results of the sorting from each person are put into a square table or matrix that has as many rows and columns as there are statements. This is illustrated in the upper-left corner of Figure 5.2, for a hypothetical person who grouped 10 statements into five piles. The rows and columns are numbered 1 through 10, to represent the 10 specific statements in the set. The row and column number is simply the identifying number assigned to any particular statement in the list of original brainstormed statements. The cells indicate whether, for any two statements, the sorter put those two statements together, regardless of any other statement relationships. A "1" indicates that the statements have been sorted together by this sorter, and a "0" indicates that they were not. In the figure, the sorter grouped statements 5 and 8 together in a pile. Therefore, in the table the row 5, column 8 and row 8, column 5 entries are "1."

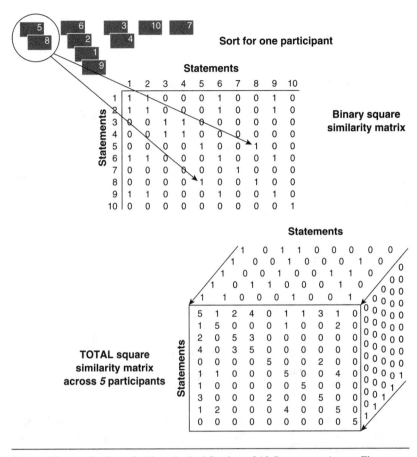

Figure 5.2   Coding of a Hypothetical Sorting of 10 Statements Across Five
                  Participants

Because statement 5 was not grouped with statement 6, the row 5, column 6
and row 6, column 5 entries are "0." And, because a statement is always placed
in the same pile as itself, the diagonals of the matrix (row 1 and column1, row
2 and column 2, etc.) always have a value of "1." This individual matrix is
termed a *binary symmetric similarity matrix* because it is a *matrix* that has only
0s or 1s (*binary*), has top and bottom triangles (above and below the diagonal)
that are mirror images of each other (*symmetric*), and has values such that
higher numerical values (i.e., 1s) indicate greater *similarity*.

After the sorting matrix for each participant is constructed, each cell is summed across these matrices to include all participants, and produces a combined group similarity matrix, as shown in the lower-right corner of Figure 5.2 (Coxon, 1999; Weller & Romney, 1988). This matrix also has as many rows and columns as there are statements. Here, however, the value in the matrix for any pair of statements indicates *how many people* placed that pair of statements together in a pile, regardless of what the pile meant to each person or what other statements were or were not in that pile. Values along the diagonal are equal to the total number of people who did the sorting task. Thus, in this square group similarity matrix, values can range from zero to the number of sorting participants. This final similarity matrix shows how all the participants grouped the statements. A high value in this matrix indicates that more of the participants put that pair of statements together in a pile and implies that the statements are conceptually similar in some way. A lower value indicates that the statement pair was put together in the same pile by fewer people and implies that they are conceptually less similar.

This description illustrates the construction of the similarity matrix as involving construction of separate binary matrices and their aggregation into a single total matrix, but this would be an inefficient way to accomplish the aggregation. In order to construct the similarity matrix from typical rectangular data matrices, the analyst must use either software designed for that purpose (Concept Systems Incorporated, 2004) or general statistical software to accomplish the task. If the input sort data matrix has sorters as rows and statements as columns, and the cells consist of the pile number (arbitrarily assigned from 1 to the number of piles for each person), one needs to develop a simple program that constricts the 0,1 matrix for each person. For instance, for the single 10-item sort in the upper left of Figure 5.2, the sorter created five piles with the following statement in each:

Pile 1: 5, 8

Pile 2: 6, 2, 1, 9

Pile 3: 3, 4

Pile 4: 10

Pile 5: 7

The first row in the matrix would give the pile numbers for the 10 statements for this sorter:

	1	2	3	4	5	6	7	8	9	10
Sorter 1	2	2	3	3	1	2	5	1	2	4
Sorter 2										
Sorter 3										

The trick from here is to transform this single sorter's data into the binary square similarity matrix shown above. This could be done with a simple computer program that reads each value in each row and determines which other statements have the same value. For instance, in our example both statement 5 and 8 have the same value—pile 1. The program would have to increment the row 5, column 8 cell and the row 8, column 5 cell in the result matrix. Once this matrix is created for a single sorter, it can be cumulatively added for multiple sorters to create the total similarity matrix. For efficiency, because the top and bottom triangles of the similarity matrices are mirror images, most computer programs store only one or the other.

Multidimensional Scaling

For the next step of the core analysis, we conduct a two-dimensional nonmetric multidimensional scaling of the similarity matrix obtained by aggregating the sort data. Nonmetric multidimensional scaling is a general technique that represents any similarity or dissimilarity matrix in any number of dimensions as distances between the original items in the matrix. A good introductory discussion of multidimensional scaling can be found in Kruskal & Wish (1978), and a more technical description of the algorithm used is given in Davison (1983).

To illustrate the process and functions of multidimensional scaling, a geographic example is useful. With a geographical map of the United States in hand, imagine that we want to construct a table of distances between three major cities, say New York, Chicago, and Los Angeles. Figure 5.3 shows that this is relatively easy to accomplish by measuring the ruler distances between each pair of cities on the map and noting them in a 3 × 3 table of distances.

However, consider how we would proceed if we had been given only the 3 × 3 table of distances between the three cities and were asked to draw a "map" that located the three cities on it as points in a way that fairly represented the relative distances in the table. This is illustrated in Figure 5.4. At the top of the figure is the matrix of distances between the three cities that we measured with a ruler in Figure 5.3. To depict these as a map of points, we first

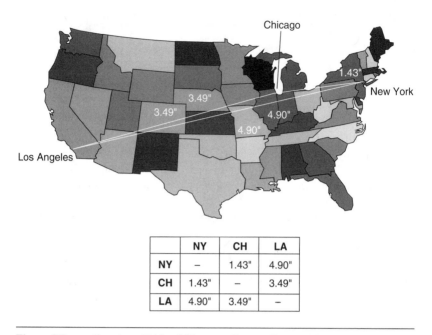

	NY	CH	LA
NY	–	1.43"	4.90"
CH	1.43"	–	3.49"
LA	4.90"	3.49"	–

Figure 5.3   Creating a Table of Distances From a Geographic Map

place two of the points (cities) arbitrarily anywhere on a page. In the figure we show LA and NY placed 4.90" apart. Then in order to place the third point (CH), we have to identify a point that is simultaneously the correct distance from both LA and from NY. We might do this using an old-fashioned compass, drawing circles the right distances from each of the two points and seeing where the circles overlap—the spot that is simultaneously the right distance from each city. The figure shows that there are two equally appropriate point locations for the CH point. This is relatively easy to accomplish if the table consists of three cities, but for more cities the task would become extremely complex, and we would find that some points cannot be located exactly.

Multidimensional scaling is a multivariate analysis that accomplishes this task for distances as in this example or for sorting similarities as in concept mapping analysis. Multidimensional scaling takes a table of similarities (or distances) as input and iteratively places points on a map so that the original table data are as fairly represented as possible. In concept mapping, multidimensional scaling analysis uses the square total similarity matrix described above as input and creates a map of points representing the set of statements created during brainstorming. The analysis creates coordinates for each statement for each dimension desired.

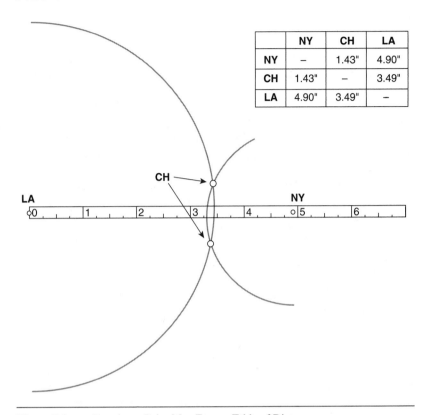

	NY	CH	LA
NY	–	1.43"	4.90"
CH	1.43"	–	3.49"
LA	4.90"	3.49"	–

Figure 5.4   Drawing a Point Map From a Table of Distances

The Use of Two Dimensions

Concept mapping typically uses a two-dimensional solution. The analysis creates two coordinates for each statement, and it is these coordinates that are used to plot the point map. In a traditional multidimensional scaling analysis, the analyst specifies the number of dimensions into which the set of points will be fitted, often examining different dimensional solutions to see which one best represents the data. If a one-dimensional solution is requested, all of the points will be arrayed along a single line. A two-dimensional solution places the set of points into a bivariate distribution that is suitable for plotting on an X-Y graph.

The literature on multidimensional scaling discusses this dimensionality issue extensively (Davison, 1983; Hair et al., 1998; Kruskal, 1964; Kruskal & Wish, 1978). In theory, the analyst may compute any number of dimensions from 1 to $N - 1$, where N is the number of statements, but it is difficult to graph and interpret solutions that are higher than three-dimensional. One view is that the analyst should fit a number of solutions (e.g., one- to five-dimensional solutions) and examine diagnostic statistics (e.g., the stress value) to see whether a particular dimensional solution is compelling. Readers who are familiar with factor analysis will recognize that this is analogous to examining J-plots or scree plots of eigenvalues in order to decide on the number of factors. An important distinction to recognize is that this tradition of multidimensional scaling places much more emphasis on the development and interpretation of dimensions than the concept mapping approach does. In concept mapping, we are typically more interested in the map not for its dimensions but for its relationality—its ability to portray the relationships among the statements in terms of distance or proximity. In addition, there is a line of thought in multidimensional scaling research that suggests that in certain contexts the a priori use of two-dimensional configurations makes sense. For instance, Kruskal and Wish (1978) state that

> Since it is generally easier to work with two-dimensional configurations than with those involving more dimensions, ease of use considerations are also important for decisions about dimensionality. For example when an MDS configuration is desired primarily as the foundation on which to display clustering results, then a two-dimensional configuration is far more useful than one involving 3 or more dimensions. (p. 58)

In studies where we have examined other than two-dimensional solutions, we have almost universally found the two-dimensional solution to be acceptable and highly useful for the participants in the research project, especially when coupled with cluster analysis as Kruskal and Wish suggest. Finally, there is some reason to think that a lower-dimensional solution is more justifiable in multidimensional scaling, especially relative to other dimensionally oriented multivariate methods like principal components or factor analysis. The great measurement theorist Louis Guttman, who independently invented a form of nonmetric multidimensional scaling, named it "smallest space analysis" (Levy, 1994) because "the nonmetric technique in general will yield a smaller space than will conventional factor analysis" (p. 139).

So, in concept mapping we usually recommend a two-dimensional multidimensional scaling analysis to map the brainstormed statements into a two-dimensional plot. Standard statistical packages allow you to specify the number of dimensions desired. The output from two-dimensional multidimensional scaling consists of the set of X-Y values that can be plotted, as well as some diagnostic statistical information. The plot is called a "point map" and simply consists of dots representing the statements, each of which is identified by its corresponding number. An example of a point map is shown in Figure 5.5.

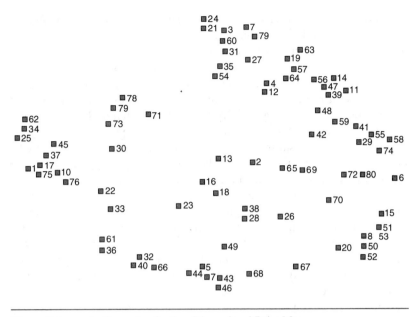

Figure 5.5   An Example of a Two-Dimensional Point Map

Stress

The key diagnostic statistic in multidimensional scaling is called the "stress" index (Kruskal & Wish, 1978). Recall that the input to the analysis consists of the square matrix of similarities based on the grouping task. Ideally, we wish to have a two-dimensional picture of the statements that yields the closest approximation to this original input matrix. We would consider the X-Y point plot to be a good representation of the data if there is a strong relationship between the input matrix and the distances on the map. Stress measures the degree to which the distances on the map are *discrepant from* the values in the input similarity matrix.

How high or low should stress be? A high stress value implies that there is a greater discrepancy between the input matrix data and the representation of those data on the two-dimensional array, and that the map does not represent the input data as well; a low stress value suggests a better overall fit. The original literature on multidimensional scaling (Kruskal & Wish, 1978) argued that it is desirable to have a stress value of 0.10 or lower, but this standard was developed in controlled psychometric testing environments where the phenomena are generally more stable and better behaved than in conceptualization. Consequently, this recommended stress value is an inappropriate standard in most concept mapping contexts. It is also important to recognize that stress calculations are sensitive to slight movements in statements on a map that are not likely to have any meaningful interpretive value in concept mapping. In this sense, it is difficult to assign meaning to the stress indicator; lower or higher stress may not suggest a "better" or more interpretable map. Meta-analytic studies across a broad range of concept mapping projects estimated an average stress value of 0.285 with a standard deviation of 0.04 (Trochim, 1993). That is, approximately 95% of concept mapping projects are likely to yield stress values that range between about 0.205 and 0.365.

The analyst can use the stress indicator as a rough guideline of the degree to which the map represents the grouping data. High stress values may imply that there is more complexity in the similarity matrix than can be represented well in two dimensions, that there was considerable variability in the way people grouped the statements, or both. The idea of stress is in many ways akin to the idea of reliability of measurement. All things being equal, stress values will be lower (i.e., the map will be a better statistical fit) when there are more statements and more people sorting the statements and when the underlying conceptual phenomenon is more simply structured and generally agreed upon. In formal research write-ups of multidimensional scaling, it is standard to report the stress value, and all multidimensional scaling programs report it.

Hierarchical Cluster Analysis

Hierarchical cluster analysis (Anderberg, 1973; Everitt, 1980) is the next analysis applied. It groups individual statements on the point map into clusters of statements that aggregate to reflect similar concepts. Hierarchical cluster analysis methods are generally divided into two broad types, agglomerative and divisive. Agglomerative methods begin with each element (in this case, statement) in its own cluster and merge them successively until all are in a single cluster. Divisive methods begin with all elements in a single cluster and successively divide them until each is its own cluster. Both approaches assume that all cluster arrangements can be arranged in a hierarchical "tree" structure.

A wide variety of hierarchical cluster analysis methods exist, and there is considerable debate in the literature about the relative advantages of different methods. The discussion centers around the mathematical ambiguity of the term "cluster." Although there is no dispute among mathematicians about what distance means (at least within a Euclidean geometry), there are numerous ways to define what a cluster is. In developing the concept mapping method described here, we investigated a range of different cluster analysis approaches. We sought a cluster analysis that groups or *partitions* the statements on the map as they were placed by multidimensional scaling; that is, statements that were placed in the same cluster would be in contiguous areas of the map. We found that using the X-Y multidimensional scaling coordinate values, rather than the original similarity matrix, as input to the cluster analysis accomplished this. In addition, we found that Ward's algorithm (Anderberg, 1973; Hair et al., 1998) for cluster analysis generally gave more reasonable and interpretable solutions than other approaches such as single linkage or centroid methods. Ward's algorithm was especially appealing in the concept mapping context because it makes sense with distance-based data. At each stage in the hierarchical merger of clusters, the algorithm minimizes the sum of the squares of the distances between all statements in any two hypothetical clusters that might be joined.

Thus, the input for Ward's hierarchical cluster analysis is the X-Y coordinate matrix that results from multidimensional scaling. The output is the tree structure, the hierarchical arrangement of all cluster solutions from a single cluster to every statement in a cluster of its own. Because we are using the MDS X,Y coordinates as the input to the cluster analysis, regardless of the number of clusters selected, this approach always yields non-overlapping partitions on the map.

Just as deciding on the number of dimensions is an essential issue for multidimensional scaling analysis, deciding on the number of clusters is essential for cluster analysis. As mentioned earlier, all agglomerative hierarchical cluster analysis procedures give as many possible cluster solutions as there are statements. In principle, these clustering methods begin by considering each statement to be its own cluster. At each stage in the analysis, the algorithm combines two clusters until, at the end, all of the statements are in a single cluster. The task for the analyst is to decide the number of clusters that the statements should be grouped into for the final cluster solution. Figure 5.6 shows a hypothetical cluster analysis for a 10-statement concept mapping project. The top half of the figure shows a statement point map grouped with all possible cluster solutions and the three-cluster solution highlighted. The bottom part shows the hierarchical tree structure that indicates all possible cluster solutions. Down the left side of the tree we have the descending number of clusters from 10 to 1. Across the top of the tree we see the statement numbers. The tree itself shows which statements or clusters get combined when we move up or down in the number of clusters. For instance, when we move from the 10-cluster solution (each statement as its own cluster) to the nine-cluster one, the tree shows that we combine statements 1 and 6. It is visually apparent that these are the two closest statements on the map. When we move from nine to eight clusters, statements 7 and 5 are combined. They are the next closest statements. The figure highlights the

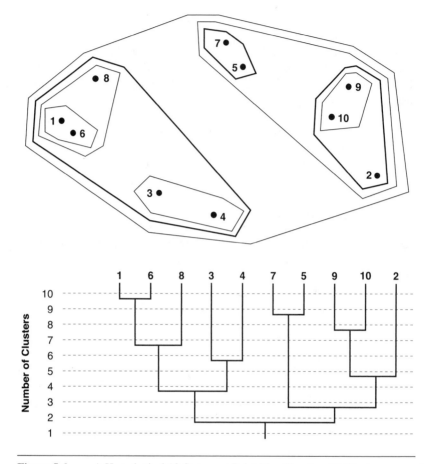

Figure 5.6   A Hypothetical 10-Statement Point Map Showing All Cluster
Solutions (top) and the Hierarchical Cluster Tree (bottom)
With the Three-Cluster Solution Highlighted

three-cluster solution. To see this on the tree, notice that the horizontal line at
three clusters cuts across the tree at the cross-section of three vertical branches.
One cluster has statements 1, 6, 8, 3, and 4, one has statements 7 and 5, and the
third has 9, 10, and 2. The ordering of statements across the top of the tree is
known as the "basis" of the hierarchical solution and is the only order that
enables the tree to be drawn without having any branches cross each other.

In the next section, we describe how one decides the number of clusters that
is most appropriate for the desired uses in a concept mapping project.

PREPARATION FOR INTERPRETATION

Conducting the core analysis yields a similarity matrix, a set of *X-Y* coordinates that can be drawn as a point map and a hierarchical cluster tree showing all possible partitionings of the points on the map. But some of these preliminary analysis results would make little if any sense to a participant group. The analyst needs to prepare and package the results that make sense for interpretation in a manner that can be used effectively by the participant groups. Several of these preparatory steps involve things the analyst does to better understand the map in advance of the interpretation. Others are essential requirements for packaging the results.

Bridging/Anchoring Analysis

In concept mapping, every statement must by definition be placed somewhere on the map. Sometimes multidimensional scaling places a statement in its location because it was sorted by many people with statements that are immediately adjacent to it. Such a statement might be considered an "anchor" for that part of the map because it reflects well the content in its vicinity. In other cases, a statement is placed where it is because it was sorted with some statements somewhat distant on one side of it and somewhat distant on the other, and the algorithm has to place it somewhere, so it locates it in an intermediate position. Such a statement can be considered a "bridging" statement because it bridges between or links the two more distant areas on the map. However, a bridging statement probably tells us less about its immediate vicinity and an anchoring statement less about adjacent areas. It is useful for an analyst to understand whether any given statement is more a bridge or an anchor because that will help explain both the meaning of each area of the map and the dynamics across areas. In some concept mapping programs (Concept Systems Incorporated, 2004), there are built-in proprietary indexes for calculating a bridging or anchoring value for any statement or cluster from a combination of the original sort data and the multidimensional scaling results. The analyst can use these numerical values to better understand the map in anticipation of the interpretation session.

Selecting the Final Number of Clusters

One of the key decisions made in concept mapping is how many clusters to have in the final map. There is no single "correct" number of clusters, and there is no mathematical way to select this automatically. Why? We use the metaphor of looking at a slide under a microscope to illustrate the problem. Thinking of the point map itself as a microscope slide you would like to examine, the hierarchical cluster analysis or, more precisely, the hierarchical cluster tree, is analogous to the microscope. We can dial the "power" of the microscope up or down to see more detail or grosser level features. This is like moving up or down in your cross-sectioning of the cluster tree, as shown above in Figure 5.6. We note that the slide itself does not change; it is the same phenomenon being visualized at different powers of magnification. There is no right or wrong power for looking through the microscope—it all depends on how much detail we are interested in seeing. Similarly, there is no single correct number of clusters in a concept map because the solution depends on how you would like to use the map. If a map to generate a high-level classification of statements into a very small number of categories would be useful for the project at hand, the analyst might select fewer clusters. If a more "tactical" operational planning result is needed, a map that had more clusters might be useful. No mathematical formula can tell you how you want to use the map results.

Another analogy that is sometimes useful, and that is especially appropriate given the tree structure of cluster analysis, is the metaphor of the forest and the trees. Flying in an airplane at 30,000 feet over a forest enables a very good view of the overall shape of the forest and how it intersects with major geographic features such as rivers, lakes, and cities. But detail is lost, and individual trees are undistinguishable. This is analogous to having a few clusters and looking at grosser features of a map. On the other hand, walking through the forest at ground level, each tree or area is distinct; this is useful for detail work, but does not allow one to get a view of the big picture of the whole forest. This would be analogous to having a high number of clusters in your solution.

There is no formula for selecting the number of clusters, but there is a process we have refined over the years through testing and practice. Typically the analyst will do this process alone or in consultation with a small participant advisory group. The process is complex enough that it is usually not feasible to do it comfortably with a large group of participants. No matter who participates in selecting the number of clusters, it is advisable to have at least an advisory group of participants review the cluster solution to confirm that it makes sense prior to using it in a formal interpretation session. To select the number of clusters, the analyst uses knowledge of the methodology and of the issue represented by the contents of the analysis, and discretion in examining different cluster solutions to decide on the one that makes sense for the case at hand. The tree structure itself is of limited value, except that it tells us which statements or clusters of statements are joined at each level of the hierarchy. Instead of trying to examine the cluster arrangement of all of the statements for each cluster solution, the approach described here capitalizes on the inherent hierarchy of the tree structure and focuses on how the analyst judges each cluster merger as one moves from one cluster level to another.

To select the number of clusters, we first decide the upper and lower limits that we might desire. What is the highest number of clusters that would be useable in the context? What is the absolute lowest number? We then review only what is being merged as we move through cluster levels, beginning with the highest desired cluster and moving to the lowest. Our goal would be to find the cluster level that retains the most useful detail between clusters while merging those that in this context sensibly belong together.

For example, with a map of 100 statements in a project designed to accomplish program planning, we think about the context and discuss it with the advisory group, collectively deciding that it would not be practical to have more than 20 clusters, and that we would not want fewer than five. We begin by looking only at the statements in the two clusters that are merged when moving from the 20- to the 19-cluster solution on the tree and make a judgment about whether it makes more sense in this project context to keep them together or distinct. The judgment might be as simple as a "yes," "no," or "don't know" whether this merger makes sense. We record this and then look at the next merge from 19 to 18 clusters. We continue to do this, recording our decisions until we have examined the merger from six to five clusters. At this point, we have constructed a ledger of decisions about each cluster merge from 20 to five clusters. At each cluster level, rather than looking at the entire cluster arrangement, we focus only on the two clusters being merged. Most likely, at higher numbers of clusters, we tend to agree with the mergers. As we move down the tree, we are likely to see merges that don't make sense because they combine areas that are perceived to have utility if kept distinct. To make the final decision, we review the pattern of our judgments as we move down the tree and select a solution where our agreement with the merges turns into disagreement. There is no one correct answer for this, and different analysts are likely to arrive at different numbers.

It is useful to involve the participants in this decision-making, but this is a difficult group process to manage, can be confusing, and can impose significant participant burden. In some contexts, this decision can be accomplished effectively with a small advisory group of three to four participants. In other cases, it is a decision best made by the analyst. In some projects, it might even make sense to pick two different cluster solutions to get at two levels of hierarchy, although we have found in practice that this can be achieved more effectively in the interpretation by doing a single-cluster solution and then asking participants to identify regions or "clusters of clusters" visually. Figure 5.7 shows a hypothetical point cluster map for the 12-cluster solution of the point

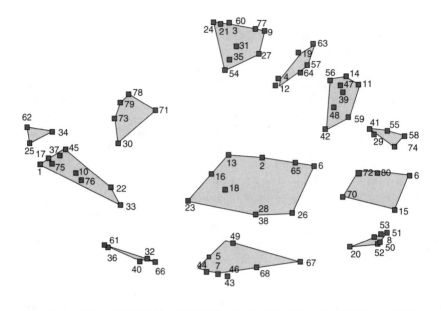

Figure 5.7   Point Cluster Map for the 12-Cluster Solution for the Point Map in
Figure 5.5

map in Figure 5.5. The decision about the final cluster solution is typically
made on the basis of the analyst's findings during the analysis, and often in
consultation with key members of the project planning group.

It is important to recognize that regardless of the number of clusters
selected, the underlying point map remains constant. This is effectively
another way of saying that the underlying foundation of the multidimensional
scaling (point map) should be accorded more weight than the partitioning of
that space into clusters. Because different cluster analysis algorithms would
yield different solutions (just as different analysts would), the selection of the
final cluster array is appropriately driven by the needs of the project and the
perceptions of those who will be working with the results to plan or evaluate
programs. The hierarchical cluster analysis in concept mapping is more useful
for getting us into the neighborhood of a final interpretable solution than as a
definitive analysis. We should always be ready to consider the judgment and
sense of the participants to refine and revise the cluster analysis results we
might suggest.

Cluster Label Analysis

Although the participants often label the clusters as part of the interpretation session, the analyst may want to anticipate that discussion. In some cases, it is also appropriate for the analyst to suggest labels without additional participant input. In any case, a straightforward way for the analyst to have a deeper understanding of the relationship of the contents to the cluster names is to examine the statements in each cluster and think about potential cluster labels. But such an approach does not take advantage of the fact that every participant who sorted the statements also gave each grouping a short label. It would be useful for the analyst to consider which of those many individual group labels might be most sensible for a particular cluster. Several approaches can be taken. The information the analyst has at hand for this task includes the contents of each cluster (once the cluster solution has been decided), the suggested labels that participants contributed during the sorting stage, and the analyst's own understanding of the contents of the map. It is often useful to look at the labels suggested by participants, especially those that match the final content well. Of course, there is no guarantee that a participant did a good job labeling the cluster or that someone who had only a slightly more discrepant grouping might not have a better label. Examination of the labels by hand could be laborious. Some programs (Concept Systems Incorporated, 2004) have built-in proprietary mathematical algorithms that identify the closest fitting sort group labels for any given cluster or even provide map coordinates for each label. One might also apply content analysis methods (Krippendorf, 2004) to identify themes among all sort grouping labels, although linking such an analysis to the map geography requires additional qualitative review by the analyst.

Preparation of Materials for Interpretation

Once the decision about the number of clusters has been made, we are able to prepare all of the preliminary materials for the interpretation session. In a standard interpretation session, we typically prepare a specific set of maps and their accompanying text printouts and present them in a preset sequence, followed by a preliminary presentation of some of the key ratings results such as pattern matches and go-zones. Because we are likely to gain insights about the results during the interpretation session, it is likely that after that we are going to need to produce additional results and revise preliminary labeling.

A key step in the preparation involves aggregating average ratings across participants for each statement and for each cluster, across the entire group, and for different subgroups (using the demographics variables to differentiate) or for different points in time. Ratings combine with the basic computed maps to produce four kinds of results:

- *Point rating maps,* showing the average ratings for each statement
- *Cluster rating maps,* showing the average ratings for all statements in a cluster
- *Pattern matching displays,* comparing average cluster ratings for a rating variable between demographic groups, points in time, or other variables
- *Go-zone displays,* X-Y graphs that show the average ratings for two variables on each statement within a specific cluster

The point rating map shows the average rating for each statement across participants. Similarly, a cluster rating map uses participant rating data to show the average rating for all statements in each cluster. We typically depict this graphically, using layers on the clusters to indicate average value where more layers imply a higher average rating.

Pattern matching compares the equivalent of data from two cluster rating maps. Pattern matching can be used for a variety of purposes. It can assess consensus between two groups of participants, consistency or change in a measure over time, and the degree to which outcomes match expectations in an evaluation. Go-zone displays are bivariate graphs that, like pattern matches, also compare ratings. A key feature of a go-zone is that the graph is divided into quadrants by the mean rating values of each variable. Its name derives from the fact that the upper-right quadrant represents the issues that are above average on both variables, a characteristic "go to" feature, especially in a planning context. For example, if one variable was a rating of the importance of a set of statements and the other was their feasibility, the "go" zone would be the quadrant with statements that are above average in both importance and feasibility. Pattern matches and go-zones use similar information, and each can be accomplished at the cluster level or for a set of statements within a cluster. However, pattern matching is typically used for cluster-level analysis, and go-zones are used to provide greater within-cluster detail. Pattern matches and go-zones will be described in greater detail in Chapters 7 and 8.

When preparing for the interpretation session, the analyst should determine which variables and which participants' ratings will be used to construct the pattern matches and go-zones. Because most interpretation sessions have limited time, the analyst usually selects several of the most obvious comparisons from the wide range of possible results, primarily to illustrate for the participants what each of the graphs can accomplish. At the interpretation session, or in discussion subsequently with a participant advisory group, they will use this understanding to identify which other matches and go-zones they wish to have produced.

OTHER ANALYSES

The analyses described above are standard in concept mapping projects. However, given the data, and depending on the needs or circumstances, many other analyses can also be usefully applied. For example, in most concept mapping projects we compute a single map for all participants who sorted. When we wish to compare groups, or assess how they differ, we use this common map and contrast their ratings. But there may be times when the interest is explicitly on the different cognitive structures of two groups of participants. In such a case it may be useful to compute separate maps for each group. In a previous project, for example, two primary groups were considered likely to have divergent views of the focus issue. Rather than pool their statements into a single statement set, we kept them distinct, having each group do its own sorting, enabling us to produce two entirely different maps. However, we had both groups rate both sets of statements for importance. This enabled us to see how both groups compared in what they thought was important when looking at either group's unique map.

In some cases, it may be desirable to examine how people are differentiated within a group or subgroup in their judgments on a concept mapping project. Of course, one can accomplish this easily with ratings, simply by contrasting one group with others. But it may also be of interest to see how participants would "map" if we look at the degree of similarity between them in their sorts or groupings. Here, our interest would be in developing a map wherein each dot is a participant and proximity indicates a more similar sort and distance a less similar one. The best way to accomplish this would be to use an INDSCAL (INDividual SCALing) variation of multidimensional scaling that simultaneously scales both statements and participants (Davison, 1983; Kruskal & Wish, 1978). In this manner, concept mapping might be employed usefully as a form of network analysis, showing the proximity between different people or organizations on the basis of similarities in their perceptions or behaviors (Wasserman & Faust, 1994).

Several variations exist for graphing maps, matches, and go-zones. For instance, the point rating map typically shows the average rating as the height of each statement bar, but it would also be possible to display other information than simply average rating. Comparing two groups, it would be possible to have two vertical bars side by side for each statement or cluster. Or, an analyst can graph a difference score or a *t*-value or *F*-value from a test of differences between groups, as was done in one study that examined differences between two groups of women on self-ratings of 100 personality items (Caracelli, 1989).

SUMMARY

Following data entry, the core analysis of concept mapping is the sequence of three steps:

- *Similarity matrix* construction from sort data
- *Multidimensional scaling (MDS)* of similarity matrix in two dimensions
- *Hierarchical cluster analysis* of the MDS coordinates using Ward's method

One of the key decisions that must be made prior to the interpretation of results is the number of clusters desired for the maps. We provided guidelines for how this can best be accomplished. Several optional analyses help the analyst understand the meaning of different areas of the map (bridging/anchoring analysis) or the potential labels for each cluster (cluster label analysis). Finally, the various materials that result from these analyses are typically modified and prepared for effective use in the interpretation session.

The concept mapping analysis is a standardized approach, but it allows for tremendous flexibility and adaptability to address different types of questions and problems. In subsequent chapters, we will show how the results are interpreted collaboratively and used in a variety of planning and evaluation contexts.

EXERCISES

Take the recorded statement sorting results from the last chapter's exercises and construct the similarity matrix for the data. Get a big sheet of paper and construct a table like the one shown in Figure 4.2. If you have 20 statements, your table should have 1–20 rows and 1–20 columns as shown below. Start with the first pile. In this example, it has statements 1, 4, 5, and 8. Now, put a "1" in every cell that has a pair of numbers from this pile (remember to put a "1" in the [1, 1], [4, 4], [5, 5], and [8, 8] cells too because a statement is always sorted into a pile with itself). The first pile entries are shown with an asterisk (1*) in the table below. After doing all of the piles in this example for the first participant, the result should look like the table below. All of the blank cells are considered to have zero values.

	1	2	3	4	5	6	7	8	9	10	11	12	13	14	15	16	17	18	19	20
1	1*			1*	1*			1*												
2		1				1	1					1			1				1	
3			1						1											1
4	1*			1*	1*			1*												
5	1*			1*	1*			1*												
6		1				1	1					1			1				1	
7		1				1	1					1			1				1	
8	1*			1*	1*			1*												
9			1						1											1
10										1	1		1							
11										1	1		1							
12		1				1	1					1			1				1	
13										1	1		1							
14														1		1	1	1		
15		1				1	1					1			1				1	
16														1		1	1	1		
17														1		1	1	1		
18														1		1	1	1		
19		1				1	1					1			1				1	
20			1						1											1

(Continued)

(Continued)

Repeat this process for the other participants, and then create a matrix that sums the values in each cell. This should normally be a relatively sparse matrix, with diagonal values that are all equal to the number of participants. Looking at this composite matrix, answer the following questions:

1. Do you see any patterns within the matrix, particularly in which nondiagonal cells have values greater than zero? Or close to the number of participants?

2. What might these patterns tell you about how these statements might be arranged visually in a point map, e.g., what statements would be closer or farther apart from each other?

3. Look down rows and columns of this matrix to examine how a particular statement was sorted with other statements by participants. Given the small sample size of statements, how might you cluster these statements on the basis of the patterns that you are seeing?

4. Now look at participant ratings that you recorded for each of these statements and describe how ratings compare for highly correlated statements. Do you find highly rated statements sorted with less highly rated statements? What do these ratings tell you about the relationship between these statements?

6

Interpreting the Maps

Outcomes are what people see. But your real art is to foresee the processes, to shape the pathways.

—From *E techne macre (Art Is Long)*, Vahe A. Kazandjian

The purpose of creating maps is to create insight—to present ideas within a conceptual framework that clarifies the views of the group as a whole and enables them to use these results in ways that will change or measure something of interest to them. In concept mapping, this key stage generally takes the form of an interpretation session in which stakeholders see and discuss the maps that result from the concept mapping analysis. The key goals of this session include participants' understanding of the results and agreement about their utility.

Results interpretation is normally a live, real-time, participatory process where stakeholders interact with the totality of all of the group's ideas and their relationships with each other:

- The interpretation session generally represents the first opportunity for participants to view the results of a concept mapping analysis and relate these results to conceptual groupings that make sense to them.
- It also provides participants with a first look at how ideas and clusters of ideas relate to each other, how they are rated, and how these ratings vary across demographic groups or other variables.
- Finally, using displays such as go-zones, this session shows participants the most actionable ideas within the clusters resulting from the analysis.

It is during this phase when participants first experience the insight that a concept mapping process lends to their individual ideas. This chapter describes how to manage the interpretation process in a concept mapping project. Figure 6.1 shows an overview flowchart of the steps involved in the structuring process.

This process includes the following core steps:

- *Prepare for the Interpretation Session.* Arrange facilities, logistics and materials, and results data for the interpretation session.

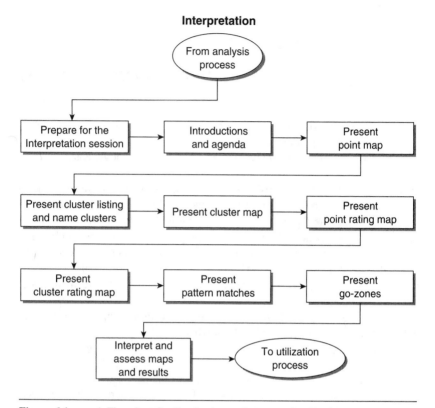

Figure 6.1   A Flowchart for Conducting an Interpretation Session

- *Introductions and Agenda.* Provide a project overview and overview of session activities to participating stakeholders, as well as a summary of brainstormed ideas.
- *Present Point Map.* Introduce spatial relationships between brainstormed ideas.
- *Present Cluster Listing and Name Clusters.* Present list of clustered statements from cluster analysis, and have participants name them if not previously done.
- *Present Cluster Map.* Discuss map of idea clusters from cluster analysis.
- *Present Point Rating Map.* Discuss rating results of brainstormed ideas on point map.
- *Present Cluster Rating Map.* Discuss graphic representation of cluster ratings on cluster map.
- *Present Pattern Matches.* Present bivariate comparison of cluster ratings across variables such as demographic groups, rating variables, or points in time.

- *Present Go-Zones.* Present quadrant displays of the statements ranked above and below average across two rating variables.
- *Interpret and Assess Maps and Results.* Lead participant discussion of the significance of concept mapping results and their potential utilization.

To illustrate the interpretation session, we discuss a concept mapping project conducted as part of a Healthy Aging initiative sponsored by the National Association of Chronic Disease Directors (NACDD) and supported by the Centers for Disease Control and Prevention's Division of Adult and Community Health. The initiative was designed to help public health and aging organizations assess key factors in public health programs to improve the health of older adults (Chronic Disease Directors, 2003). This project involved the following steps:

- From an invited group of 248 experts in the fields of public health and aging, 123 people participated in a remote brainstorming process.
- Smaller groups of key stakeholders performed structured sorting and rating activities.
- A concept mapping analysis was performed, generating concept maps, pattern matches, and go-zones.
- The resulting maps were presented at a retreat of invited participants for interpretation and subsequent use in planning.

Recommendations from this concept mapping project were ultimately used to reinforce and complement The Aging States Project's report[1] entitled "Recommendations to Improve the Health of Older Adults," and to frame a prioritized action plan.

Prior to the planning retreat, organizers invited a group of 248 people with expertise in health and aging to participate in a brainstorming activity, using a dedicated Web site, mail, or fax response. The focus for the brainstorming was the following:

> If new resources were made available to state public health programs to improve the health of older adults, a specific thing that program should be able to do or provide is . . .

One-hundred twenty-three people responded to this brainstorming prompt, generating a total of 489 statements. Members of the project's steering committee subsequently used criteria including relevance, clarity, and redundancy to create a final set of 98 statements. Forty key stakeholders were then asked to sort this final statement set using a Web site. The original participant group was then subsequently asked to rate each of these 98 statements along the dimensions of *importance* and *impact,* using a 1–5 response format.

In this example, we will use materials from this interpretation session and the resulting interpreted maps to illustrate the concepts behind a typical interpretation session.

PREPARE FOR THE INTERPRETATION SESSION

Table 6.1 provides a checklist of the preparatory steps, including the necessary equipment, materials, and mapping results that are usually required.

Many of these items are similar to those recommended for the generation and structuring sessions. The facilitator informs the participants of the time and place of the session and selects a method of presenting the results. To present the results to the group so that the participants can interpret the maps, the facilitator may use either a computer projector or an overhead projector with transparencies of the maps, the latter allowing him or her to write the group labels and other distinctions directly on the overheads for all to see. For small groups, it is appropriate to have paper copies of all of the materials available for each participant so that each person can record the group's interpretations on his or her own copies. Again, it is important to have a backup procedure ready in case of any audiovisual mishaps—the "Murphy's Law" of projection equipment can occur during this session. Having a projector and using paper materials, including newsprint, for backup is usually sufficient.

The primary concept mapping materials needed for the interpretation session are as follows:

1. *The Statement List.* The original list of brainstormed statements, each of which is shown with an identifying number.
2. *The Cluster List.* A listing of the statements as they were grouped into clusters by the cluster analysis.
3. *The Point Map.* The numbered point map, which shows the statements as they were placed by multidimensional scaling.
4. *The Cluster Map.* The cluster map, which shows how statements were grouped by the cluster analysis.
5. *The Point Rating Map.* The numbered point map with average statement ratings overlaid.
6. *The Cluster Rating Map.* The cluster map with average cluster ratings overlaid.

Table 6.1
A Checklist for Preparing for an Interpretation Session

Task	Person Assigned	Completion Date
Advance Notice		
Send invitation or announcement to all participants		
Send follow-up reminder		
Presentation Method		
Choose presentation method (e.g., projector, paper materials)		
Ensure that a backup presentation method is available		
Materials		
Agenda for the session		
Overview of the concept mapping process		
Statement list		
Point map		
Cluster list		
Point rating map		
Cluster map		
Cluster rating map		
Pattern matching displays		
Go-zones		
Projector, screen, markers, and electrical cords		
Pens or pencils for all participants		
Setup		
Comfortable seating for all participants		
Adequate lighting and sound		
Seating arranged so that all can see and participate		
Dry Run		
Ensure that the facilitator has an outline of what will be said and done		
"Pilot-test" the interpretation session		

7. *Pattern Matches.* Graphs comparing the absolute or relative cluster ratings, between rating variables, demographic groups, or points in time.

8. *Go-Zones.* Bivariate graphs of statement ratings within a cluster, showing the "go-zone" quadrants of statements that are rated highly on each of two rating focus values.

Each of these is illustrated in the following discussion.

In addition, it is desirable to have an agenda for all participants, a brief reorienting overview of the concept mapping process, and pens or pencils available. The interpretation session is probably the most difficult of the three potential group sessions to manage because it requires more free-form input from the participant group. Consequently, it is important for the facilitator to have an outline of what will be said and, if possible, to go through a "dry run" of the session, in order to anticipate any difficulties that might arise.

INTRODUCTIONS AND AGENDA

The facilitator begins the interpretation session with a presentation of the agenda for the meeting and a brief overview of the concept mapping process and the current status of the project. The facilitator then distributes the original set of brainstormed statements and reminds the group that the statements were generated by them in the brainstorming session. For the Healthy Aging project described above, 98 unique, relevant statements were generated; Table 6.2 presents a sampling of these statements.

PRESENT POINT MAP

After the group has reviewed the list of brainstormed statements, they receive a numbered point map that graphically shows how closely related these ideas are to each other. Figure 6.2 shows the Healthy Aging point map.

The facilitator explains that the analysis placed all of the statements on the map in such a way that statements that had been piled together by more members of the group during the individual idea-sorting step will be closer to each other on the map than statements that were not piled together by as many participants. It is helpful to allow a few minutes for people to identify a few statements on the map that are close together and examine the wording of those statements on the original brainstormed statement list to reinforce the notion that the analysis is placing the statements sensibly. The facilitator should then take this opportunity to give participants a visual "tour" of the

Table 6.2
Sample Statements for the Healthy Aging Project

#	Statement
6	Seek gerontology and geriatric training for state public health staff and public health professionals.
10	Develop self-management programs, empowering elderly to take charge of their own health needs.
13	Support systems change to improve effectiveness of community health promotion efforts.
17	Sponsor mini-grants to local collaborative (public health and aging services) to conduct health promotion projects.
24	Integrate messages for seniors into existing DOH programs.
34	Support pilot demonstration programs and promote their replication where need and capacity exist.
41	Disseminate and translate best practices, technical assistance in application.
54	Support an effort to train seniors to train their peers on health topics so more seniors could be reached.
75	Add questions to BRFSS to routinely collect information about issues specific to older adults.
90	Include impact measures, such as quality of life and disability, in surveillance data.

point map and its underlying ideas and get agreement and understanding from the participants about the point map's meaning.

PRESENT CLUSTER LISTING AND NAME CLUSTERS

After reviewing the point map, the facilitator reminds participants that they grouped these statements into piles, and that the individual groupings were combined for the entire participant group. The facilitator also explains that this group-based information was input to the computer analysis, and that the

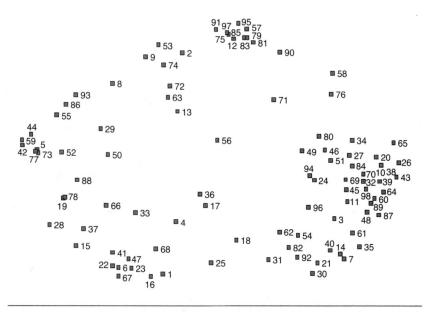

Figure 6.2   Point Map for the Healthy Aging Concept Mapping Project
SOURCE: Reprinted by permission of Association of State Chronic Disease Directors.

purpose of this session is to interpret the results. The statements are then presented as they were grouped by the cluster analysis, i.e., the cluster list.

There were eight clusters selected in the final Healthy Aging analysis, with the cluster listing and sample statements shown in Table 6.3.

In cases involving large stakeholder groups, core group members or session organizers frequently name clusters prior to the interpretation session, by consensus. However, depending on the group and statement content, a facilitator may choose to have participants name the clusters during the interpretation session. Such a process, while adding time to the session, can have the benefit of sparking discussion and consensus-building within the participant group as a whole.

Each participant is given 5–10 minutes and is asked to read through the set of statements for each cluster, come up with a short phrase or word that best seems to describe or name the set of statements as a cluster, and write their tentative cluster names on the cluster listing. Participants are asked to assign names to clusters individually or in small groups of three or four. They use both the cluster listing and the point cluster map to help make their recommendations, based on content, and to help minimize the interpersonal pressures that more talkative or dominant group members might put on others.

Table 6.3

Cluster Listing and Sample Statements for the Healthy Aging Project

Cluster 1	
6	Seek gerontology and geriatric training for state public health staff and public health professionals.
67	Ensure that DPH staff has knowledge and experience in health promotion and aging.
1	Develop or expand cultural competence training for healthcare professionals.
Cluster 2	
37	Develop/build the network of (existing) specialists in public health and aging issues.
15	Develop capacity to write grants or do other fundraising to gain more funds for healthy aging.
36	Encourage use of evidence-based program models at state and local levels.
Cluster 3	
8	Facilitate policy development at the state and local level to support healthy aging.
5	Establish collaborative relationships and research programs with SUA and CDC's Prevention Research Centers.
42	Partner with other groups within the community with resources such as churches, colleges, and universities.
Cluster 4	
56	Coordinate a public health response to mental health issues in elderly with other stakeholders.
74	Make policy recommendations based on the best available science.
13	Support systems change to improve effectiveness of community health promotion efforts.
Cluster 5	
75	Add questions to BRFSS to routinely collect information about issues specific to older adults.

(Continued)

Table 6.3 (Continued)

81	Prepare a report on the "State of Health for Older Adults in ____" that makes use of BRFSS and other data sources on disease and injury.
57	Collect, interpret, and disseminate data about health of older adults.
Cluster 6	
58	Develop practical evaluation tools for use in the field.
90	Include impact measures, such as quality of life and disability, in surveillance data.
71	Model policies that promote healthy behavior for older adults—health care, communities, institutional settings.
Cluster 7	
98	Develop a program to increase physical activity among older persons (implement national blueprint).
26	Improve access to services with transportation.
51	Identify effective community interventions able to prevent or forestall chronic health problems common to aging.
Cluster 8	
7	Run statewide media campaigns on health topics to reach seniors through a variety of channels.
82	Provide information and training on medication management.
18	Provide resources to address needs of the various racial/ethnic and/or immigrant populations.

When each person has a tentative name for each cluster, the group works cluster by cluster in an attempt to achieve group consensus on an acceptable cluster name. This is often an interesting negotiating task. When each person in turn names a certain cluster, the group can often see an existing consensus. For less clearly defined clusters, the group may experience some difficulty assigning an agreed-upon name. The statements in that cluster might actually contain several different ideas, and, had a higher cluster solution been selected, the statements would have been subdivided into subclusters. In these cases, the facilitator might suggest that the group use a hybrid name, perhaps by combining titles from several individuals. In any event, the group is told that these names are tentative and may be revised later. In some cases, consensus on a cluster name is not forthcoming, and the group is told that it can be left blank for now and perhaps filled in at a later point. A third alternative is to label the cluster with a "placeholder" that the facilitator will have ready if needed.

PRESENT CLUSTER MAP

When the group has either reached consensus on the names for each cluster or agreed to defer the naming, they are told that the analysis also organized the points into groups as shown on the list of clustered statements that they just named. The facilitator presents the cluster map and participants are shown that the map portrays visually the exact same clustering that they just looked at on the cluster list. At this point, it is often useful for the facilitator to overlay this cluster map on the existing point map (the point cluster map) to help partici-pants see the meanings behind the groupings.

Figure 6.3 presents the Healthy Aging cluster map.

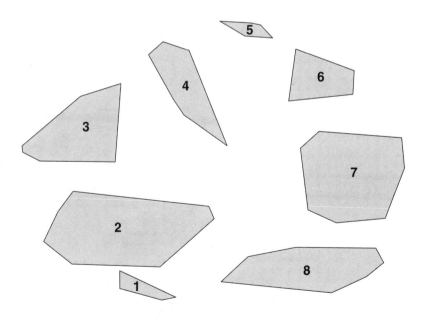

Figure 6.3   Cluster Map for the Healthy Aging Concept Mapping Project

The facilitator asks the group to write the cluster names that the group arrived at next to the appropriate cluster on the cluster map. He or she then asks them to examine this named cluster map to see whether it makes any sense. The facilitator should remind participants that in general, as with individual items, clusters that are closer together on the cluster map should be more similar conceptually than clusters that are farther apart—and then ask them to assess whether this seems to be true. Participants might even begin at some point and travel across it like a geographic map, reading each cluster in turn to see whether or not the visual structure makes any sense.

This final named cluster map constitutes the conceptual framework and the basic result of the concept mapping process. Figure 6.4 shows the map obtained from the Healthy Aging project.

In some cases, the participants may be asked to take a larger view, to discuss any meaningful groups or clusters of clusters. Often, the group is able to perceive several major "regions." These are discussed and rough partitions are drawn on the map to indicate the different regions. Just as in naming the clusters, the group then attempts to arrive at a consensus on names for these regions.

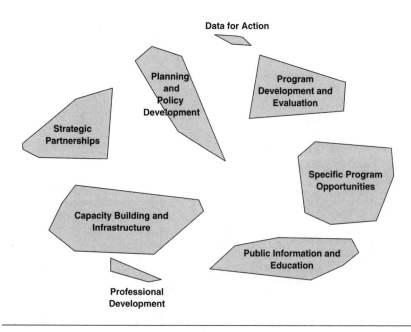

Figure 6.4   Final Named Cluster Map for the Healthy Aging Concept Mapping Project

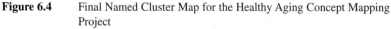

SOURCE: Reprinted by permission of Association of State Chronic Disease Directors.

The facilitator should remind the participants that this final map is their own product. It was entirely based on statements that they generated in their own words, and that they grouped. The labels on the map represent categories that they named. Although the computer analysis will yield sensible final maps in general, the group should feel free to change or rearrange the final map until it makes sense for them and for the conceptualization task at hand.[2] At this point it is useful for the facilitator to engage the participants in a general discussion about what the map tells them about their ideas for evaluation or planning.

PRESENT POINT RATING MAP

If ratings were done in the structuring step, the facilitator then presents the point rating map. Participants are shown that this is the same map as the original point map (Figure 6.2) except that each point is now represented by a bar that indicates the average rating for that statement. Figure 6.5 shows the point rating map for the Healthy Aging study.

This map represents the "value dimension" of these statements, as defined by the participants, and they should be encouraged by the facilitator to look for patterns in the ratings. Are there certain areas of the map that show consistently

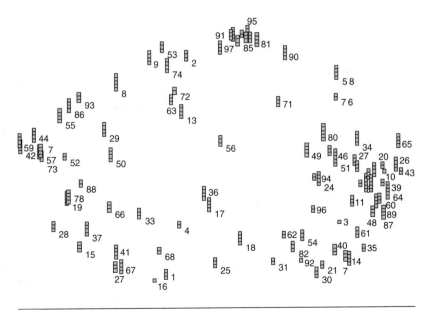

Figure 6.5   Point Rating Map for the Healthy Aging Project

high or low ratings? What does this mean for the problem or issue at hand? Usually the group takes between 5 and 10 minutes to discuss any detectable patterns.

At this point in the discussion (if not earlier), differences in opinion and interpretation will usually begin to surface. Participants may want the facilitator to interpret the results for them or to judge whose interpretation is correct. It is important in such instances that the facilitator point out that the concept map is the result of what the participants did and said, and that it is theirs to understand and interpret. It is also useful to mention that diversity of opinion is almost always present within a group. The concept map by itself won't necessarily lead to consensus, but it *does* provide a general framework for viewing the variety of opinions within a group. Participants may also begin to ask "What if . . . " questions regarding the concept mapping process. For instance, they may want to know what would happen if the point rating map were redrawn separately for different subgroups. Questions should be encouraged. To the extent that it is reasonable and feasible, the facilitator may actually use such input to construct more maps that can be examined at subsequent sessions.

PRESENT CLUSTER RATING MAP

Next, the cluster rating map is presented to the group. Participants are shown that this map is identical to the cluster map (Figure 6.3), except that layering is used to show the average cluster ratings. Participants are asked to write the cluster and region labels and to draw in region boundaries, if any. As with the original cluster map, it is often useful for the facilitator to overlay this cluster rating map on the point rating map to show the comparisons between individual statement ratings and the aggregate cluster rating.

Figure 6.6 shows the cluster rating map for the *Importance* rating in the Healthy Aging study.

These results suggest that Strategic Partnerships and Specific Program Opportunities are considered relatively more important than, for example, Planning & Policy Development or Public Information & Education. Cluster averages are not always an indicator of the rated values of the statements within them. In the Healthy Aging study, Figure 6.6 shows that cluster 8, "Public Information & Education," had the lowest cluster average importance rating of all the clusters. But statement 18 (toward the center bottom in Figure 6.5), "Provide resources to address needs of the various racial/ethnic and/or immigrant populations," was rated relatively high in importance. The facilitator should assist the participants in discussing the ratings to consider what they suggest about the ideas that underlie their evaluation or planning task.

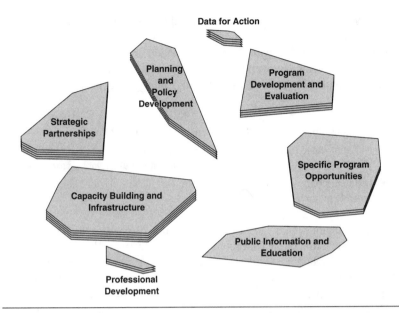

Figure 6.6 Cluster Rating Map for Importance Ratings in the Healthy Aging Project

SOURCE: Reprinted by permission of Association of State Chronic Disease Directors.

The rating data provide additional information to answer four questions.

- Although all of the ideas are important, which ideas are relatively most important? In other words, among all of the ideas, are there a smaller number of clear priorities?
- What ideas have the most potential to affect health?
- What is the relationship of importance and impact on health among the concepts?
- Do public health professionals and aging professionals have different priorities?

These questions are often best addressed by studying two additional types of displays discussed next in this chapter, pattern matching and go-zone displays.

PRESENT PATTERN MATCHING

Pattern matching, as discussed in Chapter 5, is used to show how two sets of ratings compare with each other, to address critical questions such as consensus across groups or the consistency of results. Pattern matching is typically done at the cluster level, although it can also be done for statements within clusters.

Pattern matching generally uses what is known as a *ladder graph* representation, showing lines connecting cluster rating values on a pair of absolute or relative scales, together with a standard Pearson product moment correlation ("*r*") value showing the overall strength of correlation between the two rating patterns. Some examples of variables that might be compared include the following:

- Different rating variables, such as Importance and Feasibility
- Different demographic groups, such as staff versus management, public health versus advocacy group participants, government versus private sector, or others
- Different points in time for the same variable, such as cluster ratings across two separate planning meetings

The facilitator presents these pattern matching displays to the group following the presentation of the concept maps and uses them as a basis for group discussions about both the differences and areas of consensus highlighted by them—across rating priorities, between stakeholder groups, over time, or whatever other comparison criteria were used to generate the displays.

In the case of the Healthy Aging project, pattern matching results were generated comparing cluster ratings between the two rating variables of Importance and Impact, as well as comparing aging and public health organizations on each variable. Figure 6.7 shows the pattern match for Importance versus Impact.

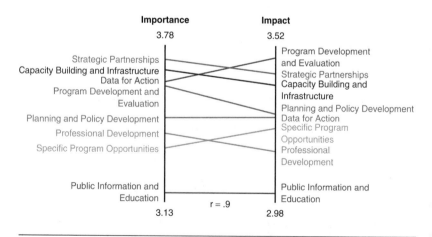

Figure 6.7   Pattern Matching Display for Importance versus Impact in Healthy Aging Project

This figure shows that there is a fairly strong relationship between Importance and Impact ratings across nearly all of the clusters, particularly with regard to relative cluster ratings and a high overall correlational value ($r = .73$). As a result of these data, the steering committee for this project chose to focus on Importance ratings only in evaluating clusters. However, other concept mapping projects often show a wide divergence between cluster rating variables, such as importance and feasibility. In these cases, such pattern matching displays provide participants with important feedback in areas such as gaps between needs and resources that in turn can clarify policy or infrastructure issues that affect planning efforts.

In this particular study, a more intriguing set of findings was uncovered in a pattern matching display comparing cluster ratings between participants in aging versus public health organizations, as shown in Figure 6.8. This pattern match showed a discrepancy in the relative average cluster importance rating between these two groups for the "Planning and Policy Development" cluster, with this topic clustered relatively high for the public health professionals and rated lowest for aging service providers.

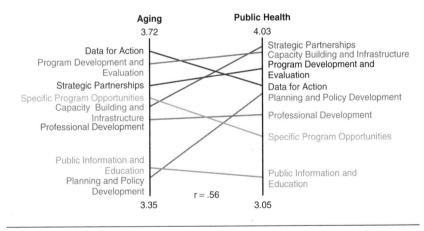

Figure 6.8 Pattern Matching Display for Aging versus Public Health Participants in the Healthy Aging Project

PRESENT GO-ZONES

Finally, the facilitator helps the group understand the relative ratings of statements within each cluster. One approach for this is to present go-zone displays for each cluster. As described earlier, go-zones are bivariate X-Y graphs of ratings, shown within quadrants constructed by dividing above or below the mean for each variable.

Statements in the upper-right quadrant or "go-zone" normally represent the most actionable ideas within each cluster.[3] However, it is important for the facilitator to get participants talking about the impact of these statement ratings, inside or outside this go-zone. For example, a statement with high importance and low feasibility might point to procedural or administrative bottlenecks that can be addressed as action items by participants. Similarly, a statement with high importance to staff and low importance to managers might open discussion about workplace priorities as part of a strategic planning effort.

Figure 6.9 shows an example of a go-zone display for the Strategic Partnerships cluster shown earlier in the Healthy Aging study. The plot shows each statement within the cluster and how it was rated for importance by public health participants (X-axis) and aging participants (Y-axis). In this example, we see that ideas such as statements 50 (Integrate healthy aging into existing categorical grants for a focus on this specific age group) and 44 (Contribute to coordination of initiatives across SHD/SUA/AAAs and LHDs) were rated above average in Importance by both aging and public health participants, whereas statements such as 52 (Provide funds to contract w/ academic institutions to develop collaborative health promotion programs in aging) were rated below average in Importance by both groups, indicating a focus on grants and public agency collaboration in this area. Another cluster of statements (29, 55, and 86) were rated above average in Importance by public health groups but below average by aging groups; however, the range of Importance ratings was very close to the mean, and within less than a quarter of a rating point from the go-zone region.

INTERPRET AND ASSESS MAPS AND RESULTS

This process leads to a general discussion of the sensibility of the maps and of their implications. The topics on the map can be now be linked to measures of interest, such as what is important, what has been completed, what has been delivered, or what has been influenced. The maps can drive action plans for the project under study, using statements, clusters, and ratings to develop tasks and assignments, establish deliverables, or set up a managing and reporting structure. They can provide a framework for the operationalization of measures for use in evaluation.

At this point in the session, it should be apparent whether there is general agreement among the participants about the meaningfulness of the overall

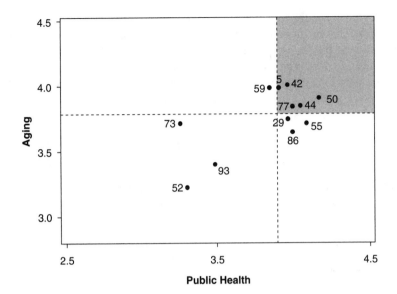

GO-ZONE STATEMENTS

Establish collaborative relationships and research programs with
SUA and CDC's Prevention Research Centers. (5)

Partner with other groups within the community with resources such
as churches, colleges, and Universities. (42)

Contribute to coordination of initiatives across SHD/SUA/AAAs and
LHDs. (44)

Integrate health aging into existing categorical grants for a focus
on this specific age group. (50)

Establish mutually logical and beneficial linkages between the SHD
and SUA. (77)

Figure 6.9   Go-Zone From the Healthy Aging Project Showing Average
                Importance Ratings for Public Health and Aging Participants

SOURCE: Reprinted by permission of Association of State Chronic Disease Directors.

---

concept mapping structure. Different individuals are likely to disagree about the
placement or relative importance of various statements, and such disagreements
should not be discouraged. However, it has been our experience that although
there may be disagreements on details, some consensus is invariably evident on

the legitimacy of the emerging general structure. For some groups, the interpretation session might be the end of the formal concept mapping process. They may decide for themselves how the maps will be used in subsequent efforts. However, in most projects it is essential that at least the initial consideration of utilization of the maps for planning, evaluation, or both be included in the formal process. This topic is the focus of the remaining two chapters.

SUMMARY

The interpretation session uses a structured sequence of steps to present the concept mapping graphics to the participants and involves them in interpreting the results. In general, this is the sequence:

- Presentation of statement listing
- Presentation of the point map
- Presentation of cluster listing
- Individual naming of clusters
- Group naming of clusters
- Presentation of the cluster map and recording of cluster names onto it
- Identification of any regions and their names
- Presentation of point rating map
- Presentation of cluster rating map and recording of all names and regional divisions
- Presentation of pattern matching and go-zones
- Interpretation and assessment of maps

This process leads participants to gain a broad view of both the data and the underlying relationships behind them, to interpret them in ways that can drive both future actions and, where appropriate, a formal planning or evaluation process.

NOTES

1. This project was conducted under contract with the National Association of Chronic Disease Directors and supported by the Centers for Disease Control, Division of Adult and Community Health.

2. On the one hand, we have not gone through the work of collecting sort data and running a multivariate analysis only to have participants ignore or alter those results. On the other hand, we do not want a computer-generated algorithm to determine conceptual structures without the judgment of the participants. Perhaps the best way to address this tension is to make sure that any changes to the map that the group decides are warranted be done publicly and with clear record-keeping so that the map is not portrayed only as the result of a multivariate analysis.

3. This discussion assumes two variables where high values are "positive." If, for instance, we had measured importance *(X)* vs. "burden" *(Y)* where high values are "negative," the go-zone would actually be the lower-right quadrant.

EXERCISES

In these exercises you are going to recreate or "simulate" the interpretation of the Healthy Aging concept mapping project. It will be best if you do this with a group of people. You might take on the role of facilitator or initiator and contact a group of friends or colleagues to play the participants. If you are working in a class, you might divide into two groups—one to play the roles of the facilitator and initiators, and the other to play the participants. It would be best if the participant group did *not* read this chapter prior to this role-playing exercise.

1. The facilitator/initiator team meets to discuss the checklist in Table 6.1. They should work through each item on the list to ensure that all of the necessary materials and procedures are complete. They should, if possible, go through a dry run of the session.

2. The participant group should be briefed about their role. They should be given the following instructions:

   > You are going to be role playing a group of people—representing key public health and aging organizations—who are taking part in a needs assessment project for improving the health of older people. At the first meeting of this group—which has already occurred—your group brainstormed 98 statements related to key factors for public health programs serving the aging. These statements were typed onto separate slips of paper and each one of you sorted the 98 statements into piles according to how similar they seemed to you. In addition, you then rated each statement on a 1–5 scale for each of two rating criteria, importance and impact, where 1 is the lowest value and 5 is the highest. Now you have assembled for the second meeting. You will be guided through the interpretation of the results of an analysis of your work from the last meeting. Each of you might want to assume a different type of role—public health official, nonprofit agency manager, advocate for the aging, or whatever you feel comfortable with. In general, you are a cooperative, attentive group, but it is entirely up to the facilitator to guide you through the interpretation process.

3. The facilitator or facilitator/initiators group should work out a plan for the session. If desirable, they might have several facilitators, each assigned responsibility for a different stage in the session. Try to work through the steps in the interpretation in the same order as described in this chapter.

Do not present any of the results from the actual Healthy Aging concept mapping project (e.g., don't show Figure 6.4 or 6.7)—these will be compared to the simulation results later.

4. Afterwards, have a *group* debriefing—including facilitators, initiators, and participants—and address the following questions:

a. Overall, how did the session go? Was the general purpose of the session clear to the participants?

b. Work through the flow chart in Figure 6.1. For *each step,* discuss how well the step was implemented, any problems or concerns that arose, and how the step might have been improved.

c. Present the interpreted maps from the original Healthy Aging concept mapping project (Figures 6.4 and 6.7). Compare these with the maps obtained in this role-playing exercise. How do the two interpretations compare? Are there any major discrepancies? Why could these have arisen?

d. Overall, how could the interpretation session be improved? Would you change the order of any of the steps? Should any steps be lengthened or shortened? Are any steps unnecessary or do any need to be added?

7

Using Concept Mapping in Planning

> Thinking is easy, acting is difficult, and to put one's thoughts into action
> is the most difficult thing in the world.
>
> —Goethe

This chapter and the next explore the original reason for conducting concept mapping: using concept maps as a conceptual framework for a planning or evaluation. In Chapter 1, we described the close relationship between planning and evaluation activities. Although we discuss the utilization of concept mapping in separate chapters for planning and evaluation, we believe that there is an integral relationship between these, and that information in both of these chapters may be relevant for any given project. Even if the primary or immediate purpose of the project is to plan a new program, researchers will recognize that the concept maps may be equally useful at some later point for evaluating the program.

This chapter discusses the general concepts involved in using concept maps in planning efforts, including specific uses in planning, followed by a detailed example of how concept mapping was used to drive the planning efforts for a major public health project. We then present several brief summary examples to illustrate the varied uses of the maps in planning contexts.

THE CONCEPT MAP AS PLANNING FRAMEWORK

The uses of concept maps in planning efforts are limited only by the need, creativity, and motivation of the participant group. In this section, we look at four examples of what can be accomplished using these maps. These introduce the idea of using concept maps in planning, from which other applications can be easily developed.

Organizing for Action or Program Planning

Organizations use concept mapping to plan actions that will move the organization from a current state to a desired future state. Concept mapping gives a natural order for action planning groups because it is a framework for dividing the planning effort into more manageable subtopics or tasks to be examined by a specific task group responsible for their topic of interest. This is especially true if priority or importance ratings were included in the concept mapping, and these tasks can frequently be operationalized on the basis of additional rating-based documentation such as pattern matches or go-zones. Using the organization of the map and the contents of each cluster, groups can make tasks concrete by assigning specific responsibilities or actions to specific people. Using the pattern matching and go-zone results, the participant group can decide to divide into smaller task forces, each of which is responsible for one or more top priority clusters. As their charge, they might be given the task of generating a prioritized list of "action statements" to be considered by the entire group at some later date.

To help get the task group discussions started, stakeholders can refer to the individual statements within their cluster, and their relative values. A number of useful questions suggest themselves:

1. Are all of the statements equally related to the cluster topic?

2. What new information might be added to delineate the cluster topic more fully?

3. What types of actions are suggested by the cluster contents?

4. Are any of these actions already being addressed, either partially or totally?

5. What evidence is there about the need for each action and the level of resources (e.g., costs, personnel) that would need to be allocated for each action?

6. What are the neighboring clusters on the map, and do these clusters suggest any additional actions that might be taken?

7. Do other adjacent areas of the map suggest potential for either cooperative actions or conflicts between topical areas?

8. What variables does the project compare using pattern matching?

9. What actions do go-zone quadrant displays suggest? Although high-impact and high-feasibility items in the upper-right "go-zone" quadrant frequently drive action planning, note that quadrants that are high in one variable but not another may suggest needed changes as well.

For action planning, the concept map is a way to link strategy and action in a hierarchical fashion. At the highest level of generality are the clusters on the map. Within the clusters are the specific map statements, the point map. To some or all of the statements one can then attach another layer of the hierarchy, specific action steps. Each action step can have additional information attached to it, such as the following:

- A description of the action
- Who is assigned to carry it out or is responsible for it
- The start and end dates
- The desired outcome or performance target
- Costs or resources needed
- Other notes of relevance

The concept map, then, acts as the overall structure for action planning. The concept map, as a strategic picture, effectively links strategy and action operationally. With the actions and tasks described, it would be a simple matter to devise a multilevel hierarchical relational database that would store all of this information and track progress. It would also be possible, given the appropriate technology, to construct a Web site using the map as a visual organizing device for action planning. Clicking on a cluster opens the statements. Clicking on a statement can open a list of the actions and their details.

The same approach can be followed to accomplish program planning. On a map that has been developed to describe all of the desirable components or elements to include in a program, the clusters categorize those elements and the statements describe them. A researcher or facilitator may work with the group to attach specific details of program operationalization—such as description of program protocols or strategic considerations—to priority statements. This approach to linking maps with detailing information is useful in almost any planning context, including strategic planning, curriculum or training planning, and logistics planning. The concept maps provide a group-defined framework to enable task groups to focus quickly on the specific issues they must address in their areas of the map. In this way, they are less likely to be sidetracked by other issues on the map because they know that these issues are located elsewhere and will be addressed in due course. Some examples of planning-focused concept mapping are included later in this chapter.

Organizing for Needs Assessment

The planning group may want more detailed information about key concept areas after developing a conceptual framework for planning, and can address this through needs assessment (McKillip, 1987; Witkin & Altschuld, 1995). Concept maps can be helpful to the data acquisition process for this in several ways:

- If the participants are asked to focus on the needs, issues, or problems facing some group or population, the resulting map contains specific issues or needs as the group sees them, and clusters that result represent categories of need. The concept maps then provide the major categories for a needs assessment.

- The rating information can help guide the planning group to decide which needs areas are more important. The needs assessment emphasizes these higher priority concepts.

- The concept maps can guide the construction of an information-gathering instrument such as a questionnaire or interview. Here, the statements within clusters can be considered "draft" items for an instrument. The researcher may then construct a short paper-and-pencil or electronic instrument to ask respondents to rate each statement relative to its desirability for some potential activity or program component, or to rate the degree to which each issue or problem is salient to them.

A follow-up importance or needs assessment rating using the same format as the preliminary ratings can be very useful. In fact, it is often interesting to compare the importance ratings from original concept mapping participants to importance from a second group's perspective. In this way, the perceptions of needs of a planning group can be compared with the perceptions of clients.

In a training needs assessment, a concept map and its supporting results can help identify the knowledge, skills, attitudes, or competencies that are required to fulfill a certain role within an organization or a workforce. A similar process can be applied in which the clusters are considered the "course titles," and the contents of each cluster serve as the beginnings of the specific syllabus for each course delivery. Ratings taken in the concept mapping process help determine relative priority of the contents to help organize the instructional design effort. An assessment system can also be derived from the map to ensure that the instructional design development is in keeping with the priority needs of the program.

Some examples of needs assessment development are detailed later in this chapter. Some of our experiences working with agencies to develop needs assessments and action plans include public school districts' learning and curriculum needs, large energy companies' training needs for technology adoption, and program development needs in workforce opportunities for disabled adults.

Organizing Report Writing

The final product of most planning efforts is a written plan or report. In addition, many researchers write reports, research findings, and manuscripts for publication. The map can contain statements that describe the details of a research initiative, and individual sorts may organize the details into clusters. The resulting clusters may be considered chapter headings, and the contents or statements are related thematically inside each cluster.

Organizing Data Synthesis and Presentation

A major advantage of concept mapping is the visual nature of the result. For many people, a map of ideas is a stimulating, suggestive, and interesting alternative to a text or tabular representation. Participant groups can capitalize on this pictorial advantage by using the map as a backdrop for the synthesis and display of relevant data, similar to displays of rating data that are overlaid on the concept map by individual statement or by cluster, as shown in Chapter 5. But we need not limit ourselves to rating data. For instance, the concept map can be used to display needs-assessment survey results showing average responses by statement or cluster. Respondents may be asked to rate the level of personnel commitment or amount of financial resources estimated for each statement, and these may be illustrated on the map. Graphing comparative data on the concept map may also be useful if the statements are rated by two different subgroups of participants (e.g., program administrators and staff versus clients)—it might be valuable to visualize on a map. A researcher may even conduct some statistical tests of differences (e.g., t test, ANOVA) and graph the estimators, as discussed in Chapter 5.

Researchers applying mixed methods face the challenge of integrating data or results that have been generated by different methodologies. Combining qualitative and quantitative data is particularly problematic. The inherent integrative nature of concept mapping can be very useful here. In some cases, for example, we have constructed a Web site for a project that enables the classification of existing data sources or reports by cluster; clicking on the cluster presents a list of relevant results for the content of the cluster. These might include a range of sources like summaries, statistical models, or data tables.

However they are applied, concept maps can act as a good way to summarize a great deal of information in a visual, pictorial way that facilitates presentation, understanding, and agreement. A good example is a recent initiative focusing on workforce development in public health, in which a concept map depicting the competencies required at certain professional levels is used to link existing assets to the competencies listed, enabling the planners to identify areas where learning resources are available and areas where they are lacking.

CONCEPT MAPPING PLANNING EXAMPLES

This section looks at one detailed example of using concept mapping in planning and several brief examples that illustrate other possible applications. The detailed example is from a public health project in the state of Hawaii designed to accomplish strategic planning for the Department of Health's use of funds obtained through legal actions against the tobacco industry.

The Healthy Hawaii Initiative—A Public Health
Strategic Planning Study Using Concept Mapping

In 1999, the Hawaii Department of Health (HDOH) was tasked with determining funding priorities for the state's share of the Master Settlement Agreement (MSA) with the tobacco industry, encompassing a $1.3 billion settlement to be disbursed over a period of 25 years, to be spent at the state's discretion. State legislation mandated that at least 60% of these funds be spent on sustainable changes in public health, including tobacco control and prevention, health promotion, and chronic disease prevention. This law put these funding areas under the oversight of the HDOH and mandated a strategic plan for them within a three-month period.

Competing interests and priorities for the use of this funding surfaced at a time when the HDOH was under intense pressure to propose these priorities within a deadline mandated by law, making it difficult to engage in traditional planning activities across a wide group of stakeholders. This left the HDOH with the choice of either making recommendations on its own or finding a new approach to engage its communities of interest. In keeping with recent trends in public health thinking, they wished to focus on community and system change as a primary mechanism for long-term change in public health outcomes.

The HDOH chose to engage in a planning process based on concept mapping and launched an ambitious effort via the Internet involving both local stakeholders and national experts on community and system change (Trochim et al., 2004). Within a concept mapping project accomplished over only eight business days, they successfully developed a set of consensus recommendations that were subsequently incorporated into a plan approved by state legislators.

Methodology

Eighty stakeholders were invited to participate in a Web-based brainstorming effort, comprising a group of 34 health professionals and community-level agency and organizational leaders from within Hawaii, as well as 46 experts in community and system change from outside Hawaii. Within this group, a total of 53 user sessions generated a total of 448 statements in response to the following focus prompt:

> Generate statements that describe specific community or systems factors that affect individuals' behaviors related to tobacco, nutrition, and physical activity.

In addition, a live brainstorming meeting held among five HDOH managers generated an additional 48 statements. An idea synthesis was then conducted on these 496 total statements by a team consisting of three HDOH staff members and the project facilitator, consolidating similar and duplicate statements to create a unique set of 90 statements. These statements were then sorted into groups by stakeholders, again via the Internet, and rated using a Likert 1–5 scale on the measures of importance and feasibility.

A subsequent multidimensional scaling (MDS) and cluster analysis created a set of seven distinct clusters for these 90 statements. Table 7.1 summarizes the top statements in each cluster for both importance and feasibility.

Planning Results

The seven clusters identified by the analysis showed a geography of thought involving political, community, and systems factors, with educational issues as a central link, as shown in Figure 7.1. This configuration, reflecting the relationship of statements to one another following the MDS analysis, suggests that education could serve as a key link among the other factors identified by participants. In addition, this configuration indicates that perceived factors in individual health-related behaviors fall in a number of distinct areas that could be addressed at a policy level.

Figure 7.1 also indicates the cluster importance ratings, derived from the average statement ratings from within each cluster. Community and environmental infrastructure, particularly as they relate to the facilitation of physical activity, rated highly as important factors.

Figure 7.2 shows the average feasibility ratings for each cluster, which indicate higher feasibility ratings for community infrastructure, communications, and public policy factors, and lower feasibility ratings for factors such as coalitions and collaborations and environment infrastructure—the latter being the cluster with the highest importance ratings. These ratings reflected the diverse stakeholder environment surrounding these issues.

Despite a relatively moderate range averaging less than 0.5 between the two rating measures, cluster rating differences were more significant in this study than they appear because they are averaged across both the stakeholders and the factors within each cluster. A pattern match compared importance and feasibility ratings by cluster, as shown in Figure 7.3. This pattern match shows that environmental infrastructure factors, such as equal participation in physical activity or pedestrian-friendly environments, were seen as being low in feasibility but most important. Similarly, factors involving information and communication were seen as highly feasible but less important. Other clusters correlated much more closely between their importance and feasibility, and on those grounds, clusters such as policies and laws and community infrastructure appeared to have a higher potential for successful implementation.

The pattern matching findings had immediate planning consequences for the HDOH. Prior to mapping, they had been giving considerable thought to what they should emphasize in their efforts. Their intuition was that provision of information and general communications with the public should be an emphasis

Table 7.1

Statement Clusters for Hawaii Tobacco Settlement Study, With Top Two
Statements in Each Cluster for Importance and Feasibility

ID	Statement	Importance	Feasibility
Access			
2	Easy, affordable access to healthy food, safe places for physical activity, and strict antismoking policies	4.47	3.14
12	Availability of healthy food choices at a wide variety of retail, institutional, and educational locations	4.16	3.71
11	Expanded hours for recreation centers and pools	4.11	4.07
58	Availability of school sites for after-school and community health activities (low cost or no cost)	3.89	4.14
Children and School			
46	Amount and quality of physical education and physical fitness training in schools	4.37	3.57
10	Literacy	4.21	2.86
17	Joint school-community activities and/or programs to promote health	4.00	3.86
79	Encourage innovative use of space for physical activity	3.74	3.86
Coalitions/Collaborations			
8	A caring, nurturing parent or surrogate parent in early childhood	4.53	3.14
88	Health care provider adherence to counseling for tobacco cessation, physical activity, and nutrition	4.11	3.5
71	Professional and organizational coalitions and partnerships	3.95	3.86
3	Involvement of faith communities in health promotion	3.53	3.86
Community Infrastructure			
84	Focus on lifelong physical activity	4.58	4.5
75	Engaging target populations in promoting health	4.39	3.93
85	Community recognition of good health role models	3.95	4.29

ID	Statement	Importance	Feasibility
Environment Infrastructure			
63	Equal opportunities for participation in physical activity programs regardless of age, gender, or disability	4.47	3.64
34	Pedestrian-friendly environments	4.37	3.79
47	Well maintained equipment in recreational facilities	3.95	3.71
Information/Communication			
54	Media-supported health promotion campaigns	4.58	4.14
68	Information that is culturally sensitive and appropriate	4.32	4.07
28	A report card on legislators actions on health issues	3.68	4.21
19	Collateral material on healthy lifestyles (e.g., print materials, posters, visuals, public displays)	3.00	4.29
Policies and Laws			
31	School policy promoting physical activity, healthy diet, and tobacco control	4.53	3.93
39	Policies that promote healthy transportation alternatives (cycling, walking, public transportation)	4.37	3.79
43	Public and worksite policy that supports tobacco control	4.32	4.29
45	Restricted access to tobacco products for youth	4.26	4.36

SOURCE: Trochim, W., Milstein, B., Wood, B., Jackson, S., & Pressler, V., "Setting objectives for community and systems change: An application of concept mapping for planning a statewide health improvement initiative" in *Health Promotion Practice, 5*(1), pp. 8–19, copyright © 2004. Reprinted with permission of Sage Publications, Inc.

because, to some degree, such media and marketing campaigns were what they were familiar with and were relatively easy for them to achieve. The pattern match immediately called that strategy into question. Although it confirmed the feasibility of media efforts, it also clearly indicated that they were judged least in importance relative to the other potential factors that might be addressed.

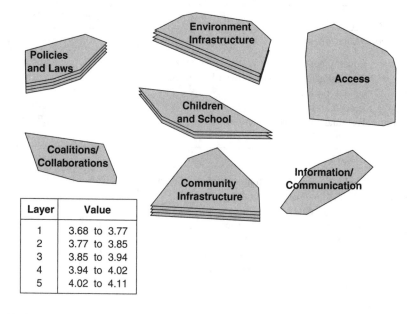

Figure 7.1   Cluster Rating Map Showing Average Importance Ratings by Cluster

SOURCE: Trochim, W., Milstein, B., Wood, B., Jackson, S., & Pressler, V., "Setting objectives for community and systems change: An application of concept mapping for planning a statewide health improvement initiative" in *Health Promotion Practice, 5*(1), pp. 8–19, copyright © 2004. Reprinted with permission of Sage Publications, Inc.

In addition to the pattern match, a go-zone display was created mapping importance versus feasibility for each of the 90 consolidated statements, as shown in Figure 7.4. This gave participants a view of statement ratings, independent of their cluster. A large percentage of statements were within the go-zone of high importance and high feasibility, with statement 84 (Focus on lifelong physical activity) rating the highest on both criteria; this statement's position had an impact on resulting recommendations for promotion of physical activity.

The structure of the concept map showed clearly how participants viewed the issues behind improving public health outcomes in tobacco, nutrition, and physical activity. It provided some independent validation that the expected distinction between community and system factors made sense conceptually to the stakeholders involved, and it further classified each of these into three subcategories and showed their relationship to the seven clusters. The map clearly

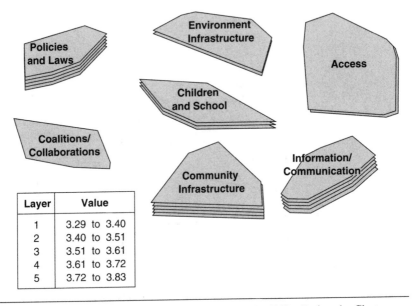

Layer	Value
1	3.29 to 3.40
2	3.40 to 3.51
3	3.51 to 3.61
4	3.61 to 3.72
5	3.72 to 3.83

Figure 7.2   Cluster Rating Map Showing Average Feasibility Ratings by Cluster

SOURCE: Trochim, W., Milstein, B., Wood, B., Jackson, S., & Pressler, V., "Setting objectives for community and systems change: An application of concept mapping for planning a statewide health improvement initiative" in *Health Promotion Practice, 5*(1), pp. 8–19, copyright © 2004. Reprinted with permission of Sage Publications, Inc.

delineates the two regions defining system factors (such as public policy issues) and community issues (such as community coalitions and communications), each of which has structure, infrastructure, and transmission issues—with education as a central component spanning each of these areas. A graphical representation of this final concept map, as shown in Figure 7.5, clarified participant thought in a manner that helped drive the development of the project's core recommendations.

The recommendations from this project formed the basis of an overall plan for the Healthy Hawaii Initiative that was ultimately approved by the state legislature and signed into law by the governor. Some of its core aspects included a focus on activity in daily living as opposed to athletics, as indicated by the highly rated statement 84 mentioned earlier, as well as educational workgroups in the school system, community-based health promotion activities, targeted media campaigns, and continuing education for healthcare professionals.

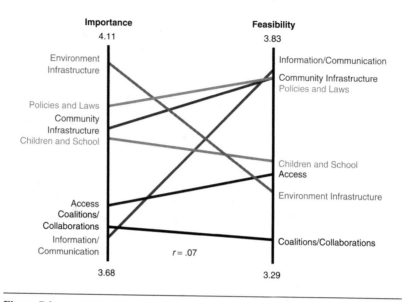

Figure 7.3   Pattern Match Display Comparing Importance versus Feasibility
Ratings by Cluster

SOURCE: Trochim, W., Milstein, B., Wood, B., Jackson, S., & Pressler, V., "Setting objectives for community and systems change: An application of concept mapping for planning a statewide health improvement initiative" in *Health Promotion Practice*, 5(1), pp. 8–19, copyright © 2004. Reprinted with permission of Sage Publications, Inc.

This project is an example of how concept mapping provided an effective framework for a very time-critical planning process, involving major funding decisions affecting state public health policy. In this case, there were several key advantages for both the HDOH and its stakeholders in adopting this planning approach:

- It provided a systematic process with a high level of credibility.
- It involved a broad network of stakeholders, both within Hawaii and on a national scale, who could participate virtually in the process from widely dispersed geographic locations.

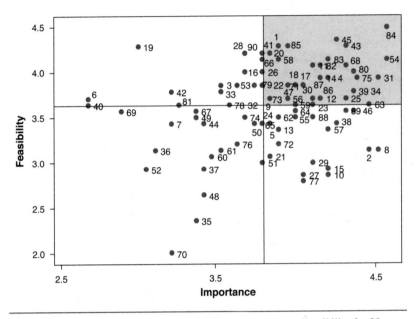

Figure 7.4   Go-Zone Display Mapping Importance versus Feasibility for 90
                     Consolidated Statements

SOURCE: Trochim, W., Milstein, B., Wood, B., Jackson, S., & Pressler, V., "Setting objectives for
community and systems change: An application of concept mapping for planning a statewide
health improvement initiative" in *Health Promotion Practice, 5*(1), pp. 8–19, copyright © 2004.
Reprinted with permission of Sage Publications, Inc.

- Its conclusions became a key part of the Healthy Hawaii Initiative plan, which
  was subsequently approved by state legislators and implemented.

This concept mapping project represented a cost-effective and inclusive
planning approach for an important public health initiative, which in turn
drove tangible results at an implementation level. The map results from this
planning project also form a basis for subsequent evaluation, enabling a synthesis between planning and evaluation activities.

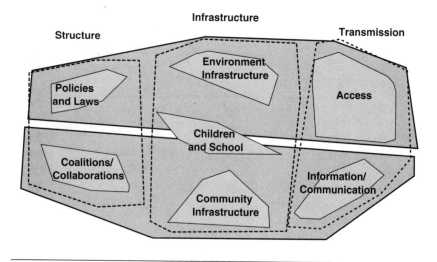

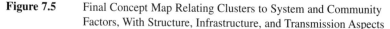

Figure 7.5   Final Concept Map Relating Clusters to System and Community
Factors, With Structure, Infrastructure, and Transmission Aspects

SOURCE: Trochim, W., Milstein, B., Wood, B., Jackson, S., & Pressler, V., "Setting objectives for
community and systems change: An application of concept mapping for planning a statewide health
improvement initiative" in *Health Promotion Practice, 5*(1), pp. 8–19, copyright © 2004. Reprinted
with permission of Sage Publications, Inc.

OTHER PLANNING EXAMPLES

This section describes briefly several additional projects that used concept
mapping for planning. We review the final concept map of each initiative and,
where appropriate, we refer to individual statements in the text.

These projects span over 20 years, and both their methodology and technology have evolved dramatically over that time. Examples include the first application of this model of concept mapping (DCL), one of the longest running
(CDC), one of the smallest (CAP), and one of the most inclusive (Delaware).

EXAMPLE: Strategic Planning and Operational
Reorganization for University Campus Life

The Division of Campus Life (DCL) is an administrative unit at Cornell
University that is responsible for delivering a great variety of services
(e.g., student residences, transportation, safety, dining, counseling, health,
etc.) to the university community. It is composed of 11 different departments

that vary by size, organizational structure, and type of function performed. The goal of this project was to produce a map that could be used as an organizing device for the long-range planning efforts of the DCL (Gurowitz, Trochim, & Kramer, 1988; Trochim & Linton, 1986).

Approximately 45 people, representing the 11 departments, were involved in each stage of this project. The focus for the brainstorming was the mission statement of the DCL. This statement addressed three major phrases, so that a logical distinction occurred. Consequently, one brainstorming session was held for each. Because of the number of people involved, 876 statements were originally brainstormed. An ideas synthesis meeting with staff and four participants reduced the items to a final set of 137. Figure 7.6 shows the final map.

The cluster map was developed, and, in discussions with stakeholders, the map was divided into four general regions. On the left side, and considerably distant from the other three regions, is one labeled "human development and values." Most of the items that fall into this category are short, general

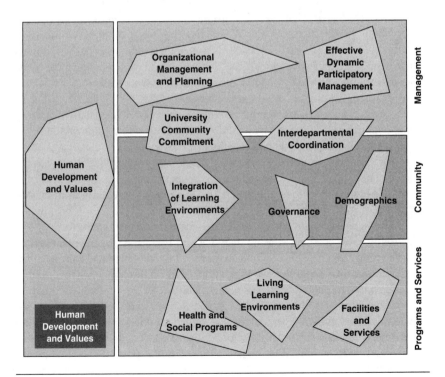

Figure 7.6   Cluster Map, With Regions, for Division of Campus Life

SOURCE: Trochim, W., "Concept mapping: Soft science of hard art?" in *Evaluation & Program Planning,* 12(1), pp. 87–110, copyright © 1989. Used with permission of Elsevier.

statements. The three regions on the right (management, community, programs and services) contain statements that tend to be more concrete or specific in nature. This left-to-right division might be due in part to the three-part focus statement (based on the mission statement) used to begin the process. One part of the mission statement seemed to call for more general value statements, whereas other parts implied more concrete actions.

The map for this project formed the basis of subsequent long-range planning and was used immediately by the reorganization committee (Gurowitz, Trochim, & Kramer, 1988; Trochim & Linton, 1986).

EXAMPLE: Training Needs Assessment for Public Health Project Officers

This project was conducted with the National Center for Chronic Disease Prevention and Health Promotion (NCCDPHP) at the Centers for Disease Control (National Center for Chronic Disease Prevention and Health Promotion, 2003). Its goal was to identify the needs of project officers to fulfill their professional responsibilities in their relationships with partners (state and local health agencies). The NCCDPHP planned to conduct the needs assessment in advance of resource commitment to create an entirely new training program for officers. It was important to the NCCDPHP that the needs of their own project officers were identified, but they also felt strongly that using this opportunity to engage other CDC Centers in this discussion would be an important planning and support development activity.

The CDC determined that two needs-assessment maps would provide the level of detail and comparison required: one map to reflect the opinions of officers, directors, and project managers and supervisors internally at the CDC, and one map to illustrate the needs of partner agencies (state and local public health agencies). A comparison of the two maps, and a customized data aggregation, yielded the final concept map that was used to frame the planning for the needed training and coaching. Figure 7.7 shows the final concept map, which links the data of the two initial maps into a common conceptual framework on training needs for the project officers.

Development of this needs assessment and training development framework involved over 500 people, representing CDC divisions and their external "partner" agencies in states, territories, and locales. This inclusive process enabled representation of all points of view. The NCCDPHP used the resulting map to link current required functions to needed tasks and skills. By far the most significant use of these results was a three-year training development initiative, linking current and required knowledge, skills, and support that the training would provide specifically to the priority contents of the concept map.

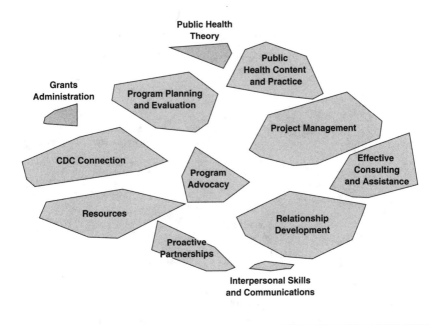

Figure 7.7   Final Concept Map for Needs Assessment and Planning for Project
Officer of the Future, Combining Data From Two Separate Concept
Map Needs Assessments

Since the training is based on the map structure and contents, an ongoing training assessment and evaluation structure followed logically.

EXAMPLE: Planning a Graduate Course in Measurement

This project was accomplished in two class sessions as part of a graduate-
level course in measurement. It was conducted early in the semester in order
to determine the group's perceptions of the major issues in measurement and
the interrelationships between these issues. Students were prompted simply to
generate statements that described what they thought about "measurement."
Figure 7.8 shows the resulting map.

The students identified 16 clusters across 99 statements. Especially interesting is their perception of a counter-clockwise pattern across clusters that
described the measurement process from beginning to end. Measurement begins
on the far left of the map with the cluster Theory & Concepts (e.g.,
theoretical framework), then to practical considerations such as Costs, on to

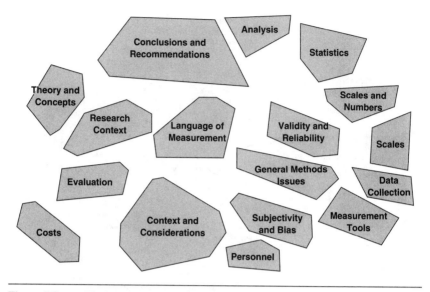

Figure 7.8   Final Concept Map for Planning a Graduate Course in Measurement

SOURCE: Trochim, W., "Concept mapping: Soft science of hard art?" in *Evaluation & Program Planning, 12*(1), pp. 87–110, copyright © 1989. Used with permission of Elsevier.

Measurement Tools & Data Collection (e.g., surveys, questionnaires, etc.), to Scaling & Numbers (e.g., ranking or ordering things), to Validity & Reliability (e.g. quality measures) and Analysis, and finally on to Conclusions & Recommendations (e.g., summary, recommendations, publishing). This process showed the students that, collectively, they already knew a considerable amount about measurement, and at the same time it introduced them to the ideas of multidimensional scaling and cluster analysis—topics that were covered later in the course.

EXAMPLE: Long-Range Planning for an Arts Council

An arts council that is responsible for fostering and encouraging cultural and artistic efforts in the county wished to use concept mapping as the basis of their long-term planning process. Fifteen members of the board of directors generated 63 statements that described "what should be done by an effective arts council." In addition, each participant rated each statement on a 1–5 priority scale. Figure 7.9 shows the final map.

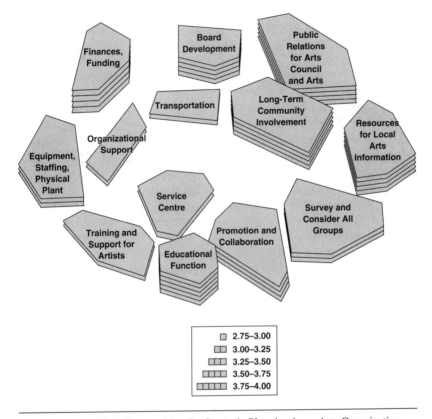

Figure 7.9   Final Concept Map for Strategic Planning in an Arts Organization

SOURCE: Trochim, W., "Concept mapping: Soft science of hard art?" in *Evaluation & Program Planning, 12*(1), pp. 87–110, copyright © 1989. Used with permission of Elsevier.

The arts council is a small organization (one full-time professional, a part-time secretary, and volunteers) that relies on its board members more directly to be active in addressing the mission of the organization. Before the concept mapping, there was little consensus among board members concerning their appropriate roles and functions. On the basis of this project, they were able to identify their major tasks as helping to seek funding, encouraging the educational function of the council, long-term community involvement, and public relations for the arts council and the arts in general. In addition, they clearly saw the need for ongoing and expanded board development efforts.

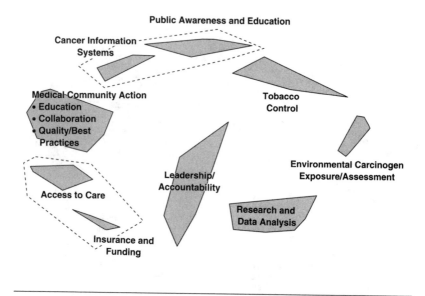

Figure 7.10   Cluster Map for Cancer Control Planning Project for the State of Delaware

SOURCE: Reprinted by permission of the State of Delaware Health & Social Services, Division of Public Health.

EXAMPLE: State of Delaware Comprehensive Cancer Planning Initiative

This initiative was undertaken at the request of the governor, who seated an advisory council to address the prevalence of cancer in Delaware (Delaware Advisory Council on Cancer Incidence and Mortality, 2002). Because cancer is a complex disease with diverse factors affecting diverse segments of the population differently, it is difficult to formulate a comprehensive, statewide plan of action to address this wide-ranging illness.

The Advisory Council on Cancer Incidence and Mortality established the following goals:

- To create a shared awareness and agreement on the range of cancer control issues to be addressed both now and in the future

- To create a structure and action agenda for addressing these needs

- To enable Delaware to move forward with meaningful action for its citizens

Applying the concept mapping methodology to the issue on a statewide scale enabled the council to understand the salient cancer control issues and concerns, as described by segments of the population with different interests in cancer control. In addition, they were able to capture the detailed contributions of various stakeholders, while at the same time summarizing these perspectives to form a clear agenda for cancer control.

Figure 7.10 illustrates the final nine-cluster map. The advisory council used this map to form the six subcommittees and to provide those subcommittees with a list of priority needs or issues, as described by the contents of each cluster. The council combined two sets of two clusters, recognizing that the concepts of Access and Insurance connected well as topics for one subcommittee, as did the concepts of Medical Information Systems and Public Awareness and Education. The central cluster was felt to be the core responsibility of the council itself, so this was the responsibility of the committee as a whole.

The council used the subcommittee structure and an action planning methodology to investigate current issues within each topic area, identify current research, if any, and identify actual or potential agencies or organizations within the state to act as partners in addressing the specific issues identified. Delaware put in place a formal plan, which received a great deal of support from the governor and legislature. It is now in its fourth year.

SUMMARY

The creation of a concept map, as compelling as the result may be, is not the goal of planning initiatives. The maps' usefulness in subsequent work ultimately determines their value. This chapter described four general uses of concept mapping for planning: (1) for organizing for *action or program planning;* (2) for organizing *needs assessment;* (3) for organizing *report writing;* and (4) for organizing *data synthesis and presentation.* There is frequently a direct correlation between the application of concept mapping results and meaningful planning outcomes, and concept mapping project examples such as the ones presented here can help illustrate the variety of ways mapping might be utilized in the reader's own planning environment.

EXERCISES

1. Discuss possible real-life examples where concept mapping could be used for each of the four planning applications discussed in this chapter: organizing work groups, organizing for information acquisition, organizing report writing, and organizing the presentation of data.

2. Take the maps from a concept mapping analysis, such as an example you have analyzed earlier, and use these maps to develop a one- to two-page set of planning recommendations. Some areas to consider might include the following:

   • How do cluster label values correlate with action item categories for the planning process?

   • How do cluster rating values affect priorities or relative timeframes for specific recommendations?

   • Does the topology of the concept maps lend themselves to an interpretation framework for the clusters, as was the case for the final concept maps for the Hawaii Department of Health example above?

   • If there are multiple ratings or demographic groups, do pattern matching displays outline areas of consensus or divergence that affect these planning recommendations?

   • If there are two rating values, such as importance or feasibility, do go-zone displays of statements within these clusters outline specific ideas of interest or reveal trends across highly rated statements?

8

Using Concept Mapping in Evaluation

Ideas won't keep. Something must be done about them.
—Alfred North Whitehead

A program evaluator can be seen as a type of cartographer (Trochim, 1999)—someone who can understand and chart the terrain of a program and its outcomes, develop maps that guide observation and measurement, and use the maps to assess the progress that is being made toward the desired destination. The concept mapping methodology is an ideal way to operationalize this metaphor of cartography. Like traditional cartography, concept mapping creates maps that can be used to guide subsequent efforts, in this case, planning and evaluation. The maps are always from a particular perspective—the point of view of those who participate in the process—and provide a framework that can be linked to program activities, measures, and outcomes.

Before beginning the discussion of the ways concept mapping can be used in evaluation, it is useful to recall the model of the project life cycle presented in the beginning of this volume and shown in Figure 8.1.

The model presents the ongoing project life cycle of conceptualization, development, implementation, and assessment. The first two phases are traditionally associated with the idea of planning. Chapter 7 showed how concept mapping can be used to address those areas. This chapter focuses on evaluation, including the monitoring of implementation and the assessment of outcomes.

The distinction between implementation and assessment in the figure corresponds to the one often made in program evaluation between process and outcome evaluation. Process evaluation addresses the implementation phase of the life cycle, and includes both the development of process measures and their use in monitoring the program and its immediate outputs. Assessment is accomplished through outcome evaluation, which includes the development of output and outcome measures and their use in estimating the effects of the program or intervention. Here, rather than viewing the process-outcome evaluation categories as distinct, they are portrayed as a continuum that encompasses the assessment of the implementation of a program, its immediate outputs, and its longer-term outcomes in one integrated endeavor.

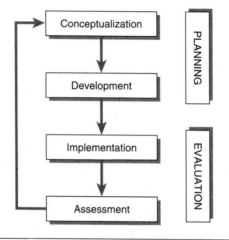

Figure 8.1   The Basic Project Life Cycle Model

CASE STUDY: USING CONCEPT MAPPING
FOR PROCESS AND OUTCOME EVALUATION

The potential uses of concept mapping in evaluation are limited only by the creativity of the evaluator and the constraints of the context. This chapter does not attempt to describe all of the potential variations of these uses. Instead, it presents a particularly rich and detailed case study for using concept mapping to develop a conceptual framework for assessing a complex program that illustrates how concept mapping can be integrated to accomplish both process and outcome evaluation. This framework was directly transformed into an outcome logic model that depicted the expected immediate outputs and intermediate and long-term outcomes of the program; the map was also used to organize the development of the measures of outputs and outcomes. The structure of the map guided the synthesis of the data collected from a variety of methods through a mixed-methods approach, and the map and logic model provided a framework for examining the patterns of outcomes to assess whether the program appears to be achieving what it intended. This detailed case study illustrates many of the ways that concept mapping can be used in evaluation and provides a concrete point of departure for thinking about other potential variations.

The Program

The program that provides the context for this example is the Transdisciplinary Tobacco Use Research Centers (TTURC) initiative (Stokols et al., 2003), a project funded jointly by the National Institute on Alcohol Abuse and Alcoholism, the National Institute on Drug Abuse, and the National Cancer Institute originally for approximately $70 million over five years, and currently re-funded in a second five-year cycle. The program is a research initiative designed to engage people from multiple disciplines in the development of transdisciplinary perspectives on tobacco use and nicotine addiction, and interventions and methods for combating them, as well as encouraging the translation of research into practice. Seven major university-based centers, each with multiple projects and dozens of researchers, were funded in this program at the time of this study.

The evaluation of this program presented a unique challenge for its funders and stakeholders on a number of fronts. The evaluation had to include everything from process assessment of the implementation of the centers through their immediate outputs and outcomes, and ultimately their effects on public health. Traditional models for controlled outcome evaluation were not possible here. For example, it was not feasible to use a clinical trials approach and randomly assign the program to some centers and use others as controls. Moreover, process evaluation alone was not sufficient to include consideration of intermediate and long-term effects; this evaluation called for an integrated approach that encompassed process and outcome approaches.

Also, by its very nature, a transdisciplinary research initiative brings together disparate types of researchers whose methods, outcomes, and expectations vary. In particular, a collaborative culture had to evolve that included clinical researchers, who tend to be oriented toward lab science and methodologies, and social researchers more oriented toward applied research methods and individual or population interventions. The centers needed to collaborate on the evaluation, so the methodology that was used had to be able to encompass broad-based participation across the members of the initiative.

The study described here was undertaken as a multiyear pilot project to explore how to evaluate complex scientific research initiatives. Concept mapping was selected as the central methodology for conceptualizing the evaluation, and for developing a logic model that could be used as a framework to coordinate the development of measures and synthesis of data, and to assess the effects of the initiative.

The Map

The initial concept mapping project involved a group of 34 stakeholders drawn from across the key groups associated with the initiative, including researchers from TTURC centers, representatives of funding agencies, initiative consultants, and other stakeholders such as tobacco control advocacy groups. These participants brainstormed evaluation criteria over the Web using the following focus prompt:

"The TTURC initiative would be a success if . . ."

The stakeholder group generated a total of 262 brainstormed statements, which was ultimately reduced to a set of 97 unique statements. These statements were rated for importance on a five-point response scale, and the concept mapping analysis mapped the 97 statements into a set of 13 distinct clusters. Figure 8.2 shows the 97 statements mapped into clusters. To give an idea of the types of statements that were brainstormed, Table 8.1 lists the 13 clusters, showing the three statements with the highest average importance ratings within each cluster.

Interpretation of the map produced the final outcome map shown in Figure 8.3, showing the 13 clusters arranged in the five broader regions or meta-categories of communication, health impacts, professional validation, collaboration, and scientific integration. It also became apparent that the clusters could be arranged roughly in sequence over time. At the bottom of the map are clusters that reflect the immediate process of implementing the initiative such as communications, training, and transdisciplinary integration. Across the middle of the map were clusters related to the intermediate structural implications in terms of process, structure, and outcomes—which, in turn, correspond with immediate, intermediate, and long-term markers for success.

Using the Concept Map to Develop
a Logic Model for Evaluation

One of the most important developments in evaluation over the past several decades is the evolution of program theory (Chen, 1990; Chen & Rossi, 1983). It constituted a direct reaction to the experimental evaluation model, which tended to view the treatment or program as contrasted against a comparison condition using a single dichotomous variable. The program theory approach involved developing a model or "theory" of how the program worked and how it influenced immediate outputs and, through them, longer-term outcomes. The idea of a logic model (Kellogg Foundation, 2001) is consistent with this emphasis. A logic model is a framework that typically shows environmental factors, inputs, outputs, and outcomes for a program or intervention, usually in graphic form.

In this project, the concept map was used to develop a subtype of logic model that we might refer to as an outcome logic model, where the emphasis is on showing the relationships between the major outputs and outcomes for an evaluation—the environment and input factors do not figure prominently. This type of model is especially valuable in evaluation because it can be directly related to measurement of outputs and outcomes, as we will show later.

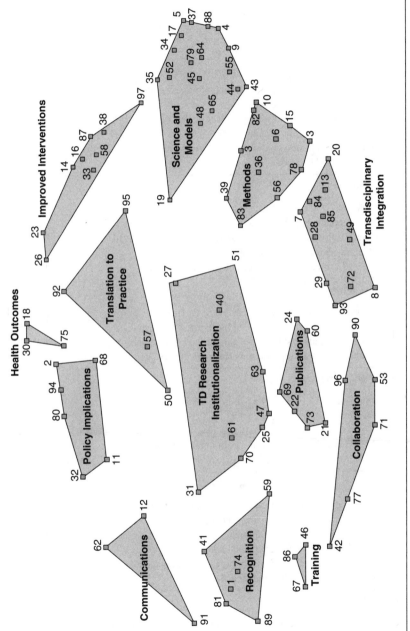

Figure 8.2 Point Cluster Map of 97 Statements into 13 Clusters for the TTURC Evaluation

Table 8.1

Clusters from TTURC Evaluation Project, With Three Statements
Having the Highest Average Importance

Collaboration	
90 The diversity of disciplines participating and collaborating in tobacco research is increased	3.86
53 Sustainable transdisciplinary collaborations occur between and within existing centers	3.76
42 Ease of communication exists both across and between TTURCs	3.57
Communications	
12 Research concerning tobacco use is more effectively communicated to the public	3.62
62 Interesting and important research findings are produced that are widely covered in the media	3.27
91 TTURC research results in frequent press releases	2.65
Health Outcomes	
18 Tobacco use prevalence is reduced	3.97
30 Tobacco related morbidity and mortality is reduced	3.95
75 Widespread understanding results of the harm to public health that tobacco product marketing leads to	2.91
Improved Interventions	
26 Interventions that are effective in decreasing tobacco use are developed and disseminated	4.30
23 Research findings were translated into successful interventions.	4.30
16 New methods of preventing youth uptake of tobacco, incorporating several disciplines, are developed	4.27
Methods	
15 New syntheses of tobacco research that integrate evidence across levels of analysis are achieved	3.86
6 Methods not previously applied to nicotine addiction or tobacco cessation are developed/adapted and applied	3.81
10 Research areas are addressed more expeditiously and thoroughly, rather than piecemeal	3.68
Policy Implications	
94 Findings from research are disseminated rapidly into policy	3.89
2 Dissemination and implementation of improved tobacco control methods occur at the policy level	3.76

11	Useful policy interventions or implications with clear transdisciplinary roots emerge	3.75
Publications		
73	Tobacco research published in highly visible and cited journals (e.g., *Science, NEJM, Nature, JAMA*) increases	3.92
69	Tobacco-related manuscripts are published in non-tobacco journals	3.22
22	Research produced by TTURC scientists has high citation counts	3.19
Recognition		
1	Research from the centers is recognized as important or noteworthy by independent sources (journal, organization, etc.)	4.05
74	Transdisciplinary research becomes more valued by academic institutions and receives increased support	3.81
41	Tobacco research is seen as a high priority (e.g., given resources) by universities and administrators	3.73
Science and Models		
4	Progress in understanding the relationship between biological and environmental factors in smoking is accelerated	3.97
17	The multiple determinants of the stages of nicotine addiction are better understood	3.86
65	Useful transdisciplinary theories or models emerge and yield new insights or prompt interesting research	3.81
Transdisciplinary Research Institutionalization		
51	Results are judged to be a greater contribution than would have been achieved without the TTURC mechanism	4.03
27	Interventions, insights, or programs with clear transdisciplinary roots	3.57
47	Understanding of the limitations of (single) discipline-based research is increased	3.41
Training		
67	New investigators are trained who become interested in and develop unique lines of innovative tobacco research	4.14
46	New scientists are trained in and comfortable with transdisciplinary research	4.11
86	More training opportunities are provided for ethnic minorities as tobacco control researchers	3.22

(Continued)

(Continued)

	Transdisciplinary Integration	
20	Tobacco control research and programs are informed by the role of genetics, neuroscience, and pharmacology in addiction	3.84
7	New transdisciplinary research proposals are derived from truly novel pilot work from the centers	3.84
85	Tobacco use and nicotine research scientists integrate research from fields different from their own	3.81
	Translation to Practice	
92	There is a better integration of tobacco dependence treatment into everyday health care	3.89
50	The process shows the advantages of linking from basic research to applied output in practice	3.78
95	New constructs deriving from multidisciplinary interaction emerge and are adopted in practice	3.65

Figure 8.3   Outcome Map From the TTURC Evaluation Project

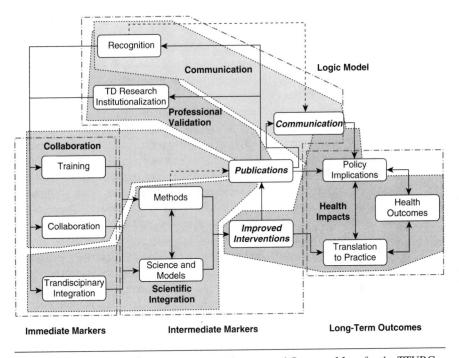

Figure 8.4   Logic Model Resulting From Concept and Outcome Maps for the TTURC
Evaluation Project

The outcome logic model that was created from the concept mapping is
shown in Figure 8.4. The connections to the map are immediately apparent.
Essentially, rotating the map 90 degrees aligned the clusters roughly in
sequence from left to right, and flowed from immediate markers, to intermediate ones, and on to long-term outcomes. Then, on the basis of the
proximity of the clusters, the likely flow of causality over time, and the
possibility for feedback, the major causal connections were drawn in with
arrows.

Beginning on the left of the map, the clusters represent both the major activities of the initiative and their most immediate outputs—*Training, Collaboration,*
and *Transdisciplinary Integration.* Ideally, these would lead to the most immediate products and outcomes, improvements in *Methods* and advances in *Science
& Models.* These would, in turn, have two primary consequences. Researchers
may develop *Improved Interventions,* and the research about these (along with
advances in *Methods* and advances in *Science & Models*) may lead to scientific

Publications. In scientific contexts, peer-reviewed publications are basic units of productivity and indicators of scientific advance. They lead to greater *Recognition* for the researchers and their centers and encourage greater *Transdisciplinary Research Institutionalization* within their sponsoring organizations (university, medical school, or school of public health). This greater recognition and institutionalization results in greater support for the centers themselves, thus constituting a feedback loop that leads to more support and, presumably, more training, collaboration, and transdisciplinary integration. The publications, and the recognition that comes from them, are the primary inputs for *Communication* of the research, and this communication is a major factor for engendering *Policy Implications.* Improved interventions developed in research contexts undergo a *Translation to Practice,* and this practice, along with policy changes that support it, are major drivers for long-term *Health Outcomes* of reduced prevalence and consumption of cigarettes and tobacco products and for reduced morbidity and mortality. The concept map provided the basis for this simple outcome logic model and the text explanation that describes an implicit program theory from the point of view of the participants themselves. For another example of a logic model derived from a concept mapping exercise, see Anderson et al. (2006), and to learn more about how concept mapping can be used to develop program theory, see Rosas (2005).

Using the Concept Map to Develop Evaluation Questions

In any complex evaluation, especially one that encompasses both process and outcome evaluation, there are multiple questions that need to be addressed. A major challenge is to identify these questions and organize them so that they can be addressed effectively. A concept map provides a useful device for developing such questions, and the structure of the map helps guide the use of the questions. In this project, for example, we used the implicit hierarchy of the map—of time period (immediate to long term), the cluster categories, and the statements within them—to identify key evaluation questions. We grouped the clusters roughly by time period (in the outcome logic model), and for each cluster we formulated an overarching question. Within each cluster, we used the statements to guide the development of specific subquestions of interest.

Table 8.2 shows the resulting evaluation questions. There is a direct correspondence between the map content and the questions. This has implications for data synthesis and analysis as well. But perhaps one of the most important features of using the map as the basis for question development is that the content then traces directly back to the participants (in this case, to the researchers,

Table 8.2

List of Evaluation Questions Derived From the Concept Map

Short-Term Markers

*How well is the collaborative transdisciplinary
work of the centers (including training) accomplished?*

- What are TTURC researcher attitudes about collaboration and transdisciplinary research?
- How do researchers assess performance of their centers on collaboration, transdisciplinary research, training, institutional support, and center management?
- What are examples of collaboration, transdisciplinary, and training activities of the centers?
- What is the quality and impact of the collaboration, transdisciplinary, and training activities of the centers?
- Do TTURC research publications provide evidence of collaboration and transdisciplinary research, and how do they compare with "traditional" research?
- How effective and efficient is the management of the TTURCs?

Intermediate Markers

*Does the collaborative transdisciplinary research of the centers
lead to the development of new or improved research methods,
scientific models, and theories?*

- What is the TTURC researchers' assessment of progress in development of methods, science, and models?
- What progress has been made in methods, science, and models?
- What are examples of progress in methods, science, and models?
- How productive are TTURC researchers at obtaining new grants?

*Does TTURC research result in scientific publications
that are recognized as high quality?*

- How productive have TTURCs been in publishing? How does this change over time?
- What is the quality of research published?

(Continued)

Table 8.2 (Continued)

Is TTURC research internally and externally recognized as high-quality research that is likely to address its objectives successfully?

- Do home institutions provide the TTURCs with adequate space, resources, and support for their work?

- Do home institutions reward TTURC work through standard academic reward mechanisms like promotion and tenure?

- Do external individuals and organizations (e.g., funders, professional associations) recognize and reward TTURC work?

Does TTURC research get communicated effectively?

- How effectively do the TTURCs communicate among researchers and externally?

- What are the major barriers to effective communication in the TTURCs, and do they change over time?

Long-Term Markers

Are models and methods translated into improved interventions?

- What progress has been made in developing new or improved interventions (for different types of interventions)?

Does TTURC research influence health policy?

- What policies have been influenced by TTURC research?

Does TTURC research influence health practice?

- How effectively has TTURC research been translated into practice (including development of written, video, or software materials; training of practitioners; developing guidelines; affecting benefit packages)?

Does TTURC research influence health outcomes?

- What is the researcher's and peer evaluator's assessment of the impact of TTURC research on health outcomes?

NOTE: Questions are organized by time period.

funders, and associates) and is stated in their language. Because they also participated in interpreting the map, the framework of evaluation questions should be especially consonant with their own conceptual frameworks. This alignment of intentions (what stakeholders believe the desired outcomes for the initiative are) and evaluation questions helps the entire initiative keep track of the strategic vision of the project, while also being able to manage an enormous amount of operational detail related to the individual missions in their work.

Using the Concept Map to Develop Measures and Scales

The detailed content in a concept map can be especially useful for developing measures and scales. This should hardly be surprising, because concept mapping has multidimensional *scaling* as its core analysis. In this project, the map was used to develop the initial draft of a Researcher Form, a survey instrument designed to elicit the opinions and evaluative assessments of the TTURC researchers regarding the entire range of outcome markers. The form consists of 25 closed-ended questions (each with multiple subitems) and three open-ended questions. The instrument was designed collaboratively by participants who were divided into subgroups, assigned specific clusters, and asked to review the statements in those clusters and develop potential questions or survey items. TTURC funders, consultants, and researchers generated several hundred potential items for this form. These were classified into the outcome categories in the outcome logic model and grouped into multi-item questions in the Researcher Form. The form measures researchers' judgments about progress on all of the outcome categories in the logic model, including collaboration; transdisciplinary integration; science, models, and methods; internal and external support and recognition; communications; and the effects of TTURC research on policy, practice, and health outcomes. The instrument went through multiple cycles of review and revision with a variety of groups including the TTURC evaluation methodology team, the funders, the TTURC consulting committee, and the TTURC principal investigators.

The form included four scales (satisfaction with collaboration, trust and respect, outcomes of collaboration, and transdisciplinary research) with multiple items on each scale. Confirmatory factor analysis results indicated that the a priori factor structure of the collaboration and transdisciplinary scales suggested by the map was validated with some minor modifications. In addition, 26 index variables were constructed by adding or averaging different items as appropriate. Finally, it also included a question that asked the researchers to rate their overall performance assessment for the center in each of the concept

Table 8.3

Items for Overall Performance Assessment From the Researcher Form
Developed From the TTURC Concept Map

Please evaluate *the overall performance of your center* over the past 12 months in each of the following areas:

Circle One Code for Each Item	Inadequate	Poor	Satisfactory	Good	Excellent
a. The training of students, new researchers, and staff	1	2	3	4	5
b. The effectiveness of research collaborations within the center	1	2	3	4	5
c. Integration of research across disciplines	1	2	3	4	5
d. Ability to conduct transdisciplinary research	1	2	3	4	5
e. Development of new scientific theories or models, or enhancement of existing ones	1	2	3	4	5
f. Research leading to the development of new research methods	1	2	3	4	5
g. Publication productivity	1	2	3	4	5
h. Quality of publications	1	2	3	4	5
i. Development of improved interventions	1	2	3	4	5
j. Institutional support for research	1	2	3	4	5
k. Recognition of center-related research	1	2	3	4	5
l. Communication of research findings (other than through publications)	1	2	3	4	5
m. Translation of research into practice	1	2	3	4	5
n. Translation of research into policy	1	2	3	4	5
o. Ability to affect ultimate health outcomes (e.g., prevalence, morbidity, mortality)	1	2	3	4	5
p. Overall management of the center	1	2	3	4	5

map cluster areas (with several areas divided into multiple subareas). Table 8.3 shows these questions.

The implementation of this Research Form itself ultimately constituted a collaborative, transdisciplinary evaluation methodology that both was scientifically rigorous and reflected a consensus on the part of its key stakeholders.

Using the Concept Map as a
Framework for Synthesis and Analysis

The structure of the map provided a content-based taxonomy that was used to synthesize the results of mixed-methods data from a variety of sources. The survey results obtained through the Researcher Form were clearly classifiable by the clusters on the concept map, because that was the structure that was used to guide their development. In addition, several other measures were constructed that enabled results to be directly related to the map structure. We conducted a systematic peer review of the annual progress reports for each project from each center (272 research projects across three years). Each project was randomly assigned two independent reviewers who rated it for general progress, for its potential impact on different groups (scientists, practitioners, policy makers, and clients), and for progress in each of the cluster categories; the reviewers also provided qualitative comments. We did a content analysis of all of the annual project report summary narratives, coding whether the summaries addressed each of the concept map outcome categories.

These three different data sources—the survey, the peer evaluations, and the content analysis of annual reports—were deliberately structured in terms of the concept map and its accompanying logic model. This provided an especially useful framework for integrating results across three different mixed methods, thus enabling more direct synthesis of results and understanding of their patterns across data source.

Using the Concept Map to Examine Patterns of Outcomes

As described earlier, the TTURC logic model suggests a sequence of outcomes of the initiative, beginning with the short-term markers and, over time, reaching the long-term markers. This pattern makes it possible to examine the degree to which the observed results correspond with expectations suggested by the logic model, a type of pattern matching design (Trochim, 1985, 1989d). In general, on the basis of the logic model, we would expect that the most immediate outputs or markers would be affected earliest, with outcomes further to the right in the model showing results later. As results build over

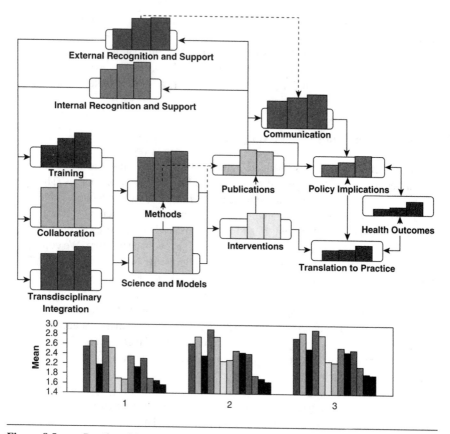

Figure 8.5   Results of Average Peer Evaluation Ratings of Progress Reports of TTURC
Projects by Concept Map (and Logic Model) Category for Years 1–3 of the
Initiative

successive years, we would expect the pattern to look like a wave that moves
through from left to right on the logic model, with more immediate markers
continually leading intermediate ones, which in turn lead long-term ones.

To illustrate, we have graphed the results for the peer review assessments
of progress in each of the concept map and logic model outcome categories for
all projects over the first three years of the initiative. These results are graphed
onto the logic model graph in Figure 8.5. For each cluster, three vertical bars
represent the first three years of the initiative. Each bar represents the average

ratings for that cluster of two randomly assigned peer reviewers across all research projects ($N = 272$, approximately 85 each year). Several things are striking in the figure. As expected, higher bars appear on the left of the model for the immediate and intermediate markers, and lower progress for the longer-term markers on the right. And, in almost every case, an increase in rated progress across the three years is evident.

Formal statistical tests of such pattern matching hypothesis models have not yet been developed, but the pattern of observed TTURC markers for all three data sources corresponds well visually with what would be predicted by the TTURC logic model. In general, short-term markers (i.e., process measures) show the greatest progress, with intermediate and longer-term markers showing lower but gradually increasing progress levels as expected. The visual trends over time suggest that the TTURC initiative is making progress along the lines that would be expected given the logic model that constitutes their program theory. The overall correspondence of the pattern with expectations suggests that something systematic is occurring that corresponds to the logic model that was based on the concept map.

This kind of pattern matching assessment has important implications for causal assessment in evaluation. In situations where it is not feasible to have comparison groups, the spectrum of outcome variables and their particular expectation pattern enable the variables themselves to act as control factors in a pattern matching version of a nonequivalent dependent variables design (Cook & Campbell, 1979). When the patterns of outcomes across variables correspond to theoretically based expectations—and there are no other plausible causal factors that would be likely to generate that pattern of outcomes—this can be taken as evidence supporting the idea that the program or intervention has a causal effect.

SUMMARY

Concept mapping can play a critical role in evaluation. These maps are especially useful from an evaluation systems perspective, where they can be used as the "glue" or conceptual framework that can guide the planning, development, implementation, and evaluation of programs. The hierarchical nature of the maps provides a structure for linking the strategic level vision with more specific action in a planning context. For evaluation, this hierarchy improves our ability to operationalize measures, structure data and analyses, and relate specific data elements to larger patterns of outcomes.

We presented in this chapter a detailed example of the use of concept mapping in an evaluation context that illustrates well a variety of useful applications. We demonstrated its utility in developing logic models of implicit program theories of stakeholders, developing measures or scales, linking data from different data sources in a mixed methods evaluation, and creating pattern matching analyses of outcomes to explore causal relationships in program evaluation.

However, the potential variations of applications go considerably beyond just the elements provided. Concept mapping has meaningful potential advantages for qualitative research as well. It can be used to develop a taxonomy of thematic categories for a thematic qualitative analysis of data (Jackson & Trochim, 2002). Or, it can be used directly with participants to map how programs have affected them. It can be used as an organizing methodology in participatory action research (PAR) studies (Reason & Bradbury, 2001) or in community-based participatory research (CBPR) work (Krieger et al., 2002; Macaulay, 1999). In these cases and others, concept mapping not only provides a useful and rigorous method for evaluation, but it opens up new models of evaluation, especially ones that involve participants—not just in generating data, but directly in the collaborative process of analysis and interpretation.

Although concept mapping has great value in an evaluation, it does not preclude or supersede currently used methodologies. Rather, it is a supplemental or alternative method to accomplish evaluation. Concept mapping can effectively be coupled with standard survey research, to enhance both our ability to generate survey questions and provide a framework for analyzing survey results. It can serve well as a useful supplemental or alternative needs assessment approach. Mapping is not in opposition to focus group approaches; it can be viewed as complementary, as providing a statistical and process framework for conducting a particular type of focus group. Concept mapping can also play a critical role in venerable methodologies for causal assessment such as experimental and quasi-experimental design. In those contexts, concept mapping can provide a conceptual and mathematical framework for addressing the construct validity of both the program and the measures used to assess it. In all of these uses, concept mapping complements established methodologies and provides a multiple-stakeholder participatory framework for enhancing evaluation. We will still conduct qualitative evaluations, and we will still use experimental and quasi-experimental designs to assess outcomes. Concept maps are useful, fundamentally because they extend and enhance the traditional analyses of evaluation data by improving our ability to articulate and test the theoretical bases for an evaluation, and by encouraging the presentation of results in a pictorial form that may be more comprehensible to the relevant audiences and constituencies.

9

Mapping the Future

How do we make sense of this unusual methodology, this hybrid of traditions that conjoins conceptualization theory and practical consultation? Where do we go from here with concept mapping? In this chapter, we take the opportunity to step back briefly from the details of how the method is accomplished to reflect on what concept mapping means, how it fits within the constellation of methodologies, and what its future might be.

CHARACTERISTICS OF CONCEPT MAPPING

Let's begin by summarizing the salient characteristics of the concept mapping approach so that we'll be in a better position to situate it in the larger context of methodology. Concept mapping is a *generic technique*. It can be applied to an infinite number of problem areas or topics, whenever people would like to organize their collective thinking in some area. The original name for the method, structured conceptualization, and the original framing theory (Trochim & Linton, 1986), were intended to stress that this methodology addresses a general and ubiquitous need. Just as a word processing program can be used to write any kind of text from a novel to a technical guide, the concept mapping methodology can be used to map anything from a theoretical construct to the plans for a party. This poses a problem. It often seems that, once people understand the method, it becomes a hammer and everything starts looking like a nail. Distinguishing situations in which the method is the appropriate fit is a challenge that requires a balance of judgment and technique.

Concept mapping is also at root a *process*. It draws upon long traditions of group facilitation. It rests firmly in the paradigm of organizational development and the human potential movement that were a reaction to the more mechanistic model of scientific management that dominated the earlier part of the 20th century. To be accomplished well, even when done electronically, requires strong facilitative skills and a sensitivity to context. It is a structured approach, but it cannot be automated. It relies on technology, but it cannot be completely programmed. Something central to the human experience of the process is essential to its value.

Concept mapping is a *group endeavor*. Although it can be used by an individual, and we describe ways of doing so, it is an unwieldy and less productive approach than other individual-use tools. Very often the group involved in concept mapping is a community or even a collection of multiple communities, and the method becomes a structured process for navigating the thinking of these communities. Thus, it directly supports and enhances the endeavors of community-based *participatory research,* community organizing and development, organizational learning, and participatory action research.

Concept mapping is *conceptual.* It emphasizes the world that we as humans construct. It maps the meanings that we associate with that world. For realists, it provides an empirically replicable way to describe the constructs that presumably have their existence in the unconstructed world outside our minds. To constructivists, it maps the collective constructions and provides a means to engage each other with them. The method is in this sense ontologically neutral, providing an approach to concepts from multiple philosophical and paradigmatic perspectives.

Concept mapping is a real-world *practical consultative method.* It cannot be dismissed as simply a statistical approach, although it relies on statistics. We can imagine creating analogues to concept mapping using other statistical techniques, an endeavor that would be well worth pursuing. But at this time, concept mapping is a practical process that is typically applied in real-world contexts to address issues or topics of direct concern to the participants. The fact that concept mapping is scalable to multiple levels and is highly flexible enhances its practical utility.

Yet concept mapping is also an *applied multivariate methodology.* It would be perfectly legitimate to describe it as an application of applied multidimensional scaling. It rests on a firm mathematical foundation and has the appeal of both independent replicability and rigor. We often recommend to users that when describing concept mapping to academic audiences, where quality seems often to be associated with academic pedigree or authority, a researcher can present the methodology without using the more prosaic term "concept mapping," and it is legitimate to do so. Description would focus on multivariate statistical techniques (multidimensional scaling, hierarchical cluster analysis), on the structured nature of the method, on conceptual representation, and so on, enabling the academic audience to recognize the science base for the approach.

For community-based organizations, by contrast, we often describe the process without reference to the fundamental analyses; rather, we discuss concept mapping in terms of group participation in the creation of a current state of the issues, or of building a community solution, or of identifying gaps between priorities and programs.

Concept mapping is an *integrative mixed method*. Rather than simply combining qualitative and quantitative methods, it challenges the distinction between these two and suggests that they may indeed be more deeply intertwined. In some sense it is a method that supports the notion that qualitative information can be well represented quantitatively and that quantitative information rests upon qualitative judgment (Trochim, 2001). It continually encourages and requires the facilitator and participants to see the issue in question from multiple perspectives.

When applied with groups, as is typically the case, concept mapping is inherently a *systems methodology*. Human and organizational systems use concept mapping to address systems issues and challenges (Trochim, Cabrera, Milstein, Gallagher, & Leischow, 2006). The results of a particular mapping are appropriately considered as describing a conceptual system itself. It is not by chance that the title for the major software program that does concept mapping is the Concept *System,* for its system qualities and capabilities were central from the start. Concept mapping is at the center of current discussions about systems sciences and systems thinking. For instance, from the perspective of complex adaptive systems or complexity science (Trochim & Cabrera, 2005), concept mapping is a useful method for enabling a group to articulate their implicit model. When the focus is constructed for this purpose, the clusters (and statements within them) can be construed as "simple rules" that connect to the model. Autonomous agents (e.g., the participants), by applying these implicit rules more consciously, may be able to encourage the emergence of new and perhaps more adaptive behavior. Thus, in the evolution of human endeavors, concept mapping can play an important role as a methodology that helps encourage learning, creativity, and adaptation.

WHERE DOES CONCEPT MAPPING FIT?

Where might we place concept mapping within the galaxy of other methods or methodological traditions? Is it an applied statistical methodology? Is it an organizational development tool? Is it a facilitated group process approach? Yes. Yes. And, yes. How we classify concept mapping and think of it in comparison to other approaches all depends on which tradition we are considering.

For example, consider how we would classify concept mapping just within the traditions of quantitative statistical methods. It is clearly a multivariate statistical method that rests ultimately on the general linear model and can be formulated mathematically within that framework. It is not a hypothesis testing approach, and in this sense falls much closer to multivariate relational methods like factor analysis, relational structural equation modeling, and principal components analysis than it does to multiple regression or analysis of variance. It is often used in a formative and correlational manner, to help aid the understanding of the potential interrelationships among constructs. Thus, it is used more for conceptual framework development than for testing the implications of such frameworks. But that may be largely an artifact of the typical sequence of things, the fact that most real-world projects cannot move well into hypothesis testing until they have a firm grasp of model specification and construct validity. From its inception, there was an emphasis in concept mapping on its value within a hypothesis testing context. Pattern matching was constructed to enable complex tests of hypotheses and to enhance causal inference. The value of concept mapping for improving construct validity was linked to its value for enhancing internal validity. There have been fewer examples of its use in this context, because there is simply greater demand for the more foundational exploratory work. Thus, although we can describe concept mapping in the multivariate tradition as having potential linkages with advanced hypothesis testing approaches such as multiple regression, it is historically and experientially more accurate to situate it with its exploratory multivariate cousins, and that is where most multidimensional scaling is placed.

Concept mapping resembles at one extreme the notion of a small group endeavor such as a focus group, and at the other a large-scale sample survey. Depending on the purpose of the project, its use is appropriate for either. It would be perfectly reasonable to describe a small-group version of concept mapping in the language of focus groups, and in this sense has a focus group's advantages improved by the addition of a multivariate engine and participatory analysis by the focus group participants themselves. In the same vein, it would be possible to describe a concept mapping project entirely in the language of survey research. Here, in addition to the traditional notion that a survey involves collecting data from a respondent sample, the concept mapping variation adds that the survey is also both designed and analyzed collaboratively by the respondents. So although concept mapping can be described as a focus group or a survey, it is a unique form of both.

Concept mapping facilitators need a broad range of skills; these may vary depending on the nature of the project. A concept mapping project in a business environment may require considerably different sensitivities and abilities than a community-based participatory one. It certainly would be possible to conduct concept mapping in the manner of much traditional social research, where the facilitator primarily collects data, processes them with analytic tools, and reports on the results. In such an application, the demand on the facilitator to have the social skills to manage the process would be considerably reduced. On the other hand, it is also possible to conceive of an analogous form of concept mapping that focuses entirely on the group process steps and, for the analysis, skips the multivariate statistics entirely and simply engages the group in directly drawing a map of their ideas. This is a process familiar in organizational consulting, and one many of us have participated in: we put newsprint (or its more modern electronic equivalent) all over the wall and, when we have exhaustively free-listed ideas, we come to the often daunting moment where the facilitator summons as much enthusiasm as possible to say "OK, now let's organize this!" In such an application, it is possible for the facilitator to accomplish this with no knowledge of multivariate statistics and no specialized software.

But the heart of the concept mapping method described in this volume lies between these extremes; it challenges the facilitator in unique ways, and can be demanding. It requires a sensitivity to process and an ability to work with groups, remembering that the result of a concept mapping initiative is the commonly authored framework of those who have contributed to it. And although conducting successful concept mapping doesn't require a statistical background, it does expect that the facilitator can use the required programs or software and has some level of understanding of the multivariate basis of the analysis.

The concept mapping tradition stands in opposition to an elitist notion of statistics. It shows that one can make use of highly sophisticated multivariate tools and meet their important contextual assumptions. It does require that people who conduct concept mapping be able to explain the results of multivariate statistics to participants. Concept mapping facilitators are in one sense translators who understand enough of two languages to enable communication, but who are not the grammarians or symanticists in either language that focus on how such meaning is made.

Concept mapping, then, is a blended approach whose facilitator is comfortable at the interstices of multiple traditions, and in that sense is interdisciplinary. To the extent that the concept mapping methodology is a unique blending of statistics, measurement and scaling, and organizational development methods, the facilitator might even legitimately be termed transdisciplinary (Stokols et al., 2003). Concept mapping combines the systematic and rigorous approaches of science with the sensitivities and judgments of the arts. It is perhaps best situated as both a "soft science" and a "hard art" (Trochim, 1989b) in the idealistic sense that recognizes that science is always and inherently a human endeavor and art is always a form of discipline.

Ultimately, concept mapping is a unique methodology. Although it has numerous cousins on the evolutionary tree of methodology, they are at some level not a close-knit family. Although each of the salient elements in concept mapping comes from well-known traditions, the unique dynamic integration of them into a whole methodology makes it different from its pieces. In a very real sense the whole of concept mapping is greater than the sum of its parts.

THE PATH AHEAD

This is a very exciting time in the development of the concept mapping methodology. One of the major changes over the past 20 years has been the evolution of the Internet and associated technologies as an integral part of our world. Groups and nations that had limited access in the early days of the Internet are likely to have sufficient access in the near future so that they will not be excluded from processes that rely on it. This opens the door to methods of communicating and interacting that simply could not exist previously.

We have already made great strides in moving concept mapping technologies into a Web environment, and this is clearly a major direction for this methodology as it evolves. It is already relatively easy to construct a project that enables worldwide participation under a common project schedule that still enables asynchronous individual participation as desired. At the same time, and with the same technology, a facilitator can work in a single room with a group of 15 or 20 people who accomplish the process entirely face to face without the participants ever directly using technology.

This broad range of scalability and flexibility will characterize concept mapping in the years ahead even more than it has to date. In addition to the obvious and daunting issues of multiple languages, perhaps the major challenge is in how to try to achieve the reach of global scale and the intimacy of the local or community setting. The best concept mapping projects blend the "high tech" use of computers for communication and analysis with the "high touch" engagement of face-to-face encounter. This dual challenge is not likely to be addressed with technologies alone, however sophisticated. There will always be a need for direct human encounter that will not be easily mitigated with even the most sophisticated of anticipated technologies. This balancing of the technological and the human has always been at the center of the concept mapping endeavor. And although the specific technological forms and human process issues will evolve, the tension and need to balance these two forces will certainly be at the heart of concept mapping well into the future.

Appendix

Concept Mapping Dissertations

Abstracts of these dissertations are available at http://www.conceptsystems.com/ dissertations.

Abrahams, D. A. (2004). Technology adoption in higher education: A framework for identifying and prioritizing issues and barriers to adoption. Ph.D. dissertation, Cornell University.

Antonucci, S. R. (2004). Counselling processes experienced by adult male survivors of childhood sexual abuse. Ph.D. dissertation, University of Alberta, Canada.

Barakett, L. A. M. (1999). The latent organization of salient memories: A psychoanalytic perspective (psychoanalytic theory, concept mapping). Ph.D. dissertation, Auburn University.

Bedi, R. P. (2004). Concept-mapping the client's perspective on counselling alliance formation. Ph.D. dissertation, University of British Columbia, Canada.

Bosch, S. J. (2004). Identifying relevant variables for understanding how school facilities affect educational outcomes. Ph.D. dissertation, Georgia Institute of Technology.

Brossard, D. (2002). Media effects, public perceptions of science and authoritarian attitudes towards agricultural biotechnology decision-making. Ph.D. dissertation, Cornell University.

Brown, J. B. (1999). Traumatic sequalae in Vietnam veterans: A concept map. Ph.D. dissertation, Auburn University.

Cabrera, D. (2006). Crisis of conceptualization: The challenges of systems thinking in public health. Ph.D. dissertation, Cornell University.

Cacy, J. R. (1995). The reality of stakeholder groups: A study of the validity and reliability of concept maps. Ph.D. dissertation, University of Oklahoma.

Chun, J. (2004). Stress and coping strategies in runaway youths: An application of concept mapping. Ph.D. dissertation, University of Texas at Austin.

Clayton, L. B. (2002). The use of concept mapping to evaluate the isomorphism of the hierarchical leisure constraint typology. Ph.D. dissertation, Clemson University.

Davidson, M. L. (2000). Using moral maxims to promote character development in sixth-grade students: A collaborative action research approach for planning, implementing, and evaluating comprehensive character education strategies. Ph.D. dissertation, Cornell University.

Davis, T. S. (2003). Viability of concept mapping for assessing cultural competence in children's mental health systems of care: A comparison of theoretical and community conceptualizations. Ph.D. dissertation, University of Texas at Austin.

Davis, T. S. K. (1994). Job search activities: A comparison of predicted and observed search patterns of structurally unemployed job seekers. Ph.D. dissertation, Cornell University.

Diehl, D. C. (2000). Emergent literacy and parent-child reading in Head Start families: The implementation and evaluation of a multigenerational reading program. Ph.D. dissertation, Cornell University.

Driebe, N. M. (2000). The devolution challenge: A case study of Americorps. Ph.D. dissertation, Cornell University.

Dumont, J. M. (1993). Community living and psychiatric hospitalization from a consumer/survivor perspective: A causal concept mapping approach. Ph.D. dissertation, Cornell University.

Edwards, A. E. (2002). Mobilizing the village: Collaborating with parents and community members to increase parental involvement in a high school of the arts. Ph.D. dissertation, Georgia State University.

Florio, G. A. (1997). The structure of work-related stress and coping among oncology nurses on high-stress units: A transactional analysis. Ph.D. dissertation, State University of New York at Buffalo.

Gannon, E. J. (2002). Men's perceptions of the ideal woman: A concept map. Ph.D. dissertation, Auburn University.

Gans, J. (2000). Facilitating synthesis and advancing methodological development in strategic planning. Ph.D. dissertation, Cornell University.

Gol, A. R. (1994). Coping theories and their underlying dimensions: A reevaluation using concept mapping. Ph.D. dissertation, Texas Tech University.

Grant, L. C. (1997). Impact of multiple sclerosis on marital life. Ph.D. dissertation, University of Alberta, Canada.

Grayson, T. E. (1992). Identifying program theory: A step toward evaluating categorical state-funded educational programs. Ph.D. dissertation, University of Illinois at Urbana-Champaign.

Harper, R. L., Jr. (2001). The professionalization of logistics: A management specialty to meet 21st century challenges. Ph.D. dissertation, Nova Southeastern University.

Harris, K. D. (2004). The lived experience of perceived stress in the lives of black women. Ph.D. dissertation, D'Youville College.

Hawkins, B. (2003). Rehabilitation services to youths and adults with visual disabilities: What is critical? Ph.D. dissertation, Cornell University.

Hayward, G. B. (2002). Developing a competency model-based maintenance manager qualification program utilizing concept mapping methodology. Ph.D. dissertation, Capella University.

Jackson, K. M. (2003). The team exchange contract in autonomous work groups: Behaviors and work strategies for sustainable performance. Ph.D. dissertation, Cornell University.

Johnson, J. M. (2003). Barriers to racial/ethnic minority participation in medical research: A comparison of community defined barriers and health professional perceptions. Ph.D. dissertation, Cornell University.

Johnston, H. (1997). Piecing together the "mosaic" called diversity: One community college's experience with hiring a more diverse faculty. Ph.D. dissertation, University of Illinois at Urbana-Champaign.

Joseph, D. D. (2004). Hispanic dropouts speak out: A study of Hispanic youth and their experiences in the public school system. Ph.D. dissertation, The University of Texas at Austin.

Klostermann, K. C. (2003). Adolescent suicidal behavior: Causes and prevention. Ph.D. dissertation, State University of New York at Buffalo.

Kohler, P. D. (1993). Serving students with disabilities in postsecondary education settings: A conceptual framework of program outcomes. Ph.D. dissertation, University of Illinois at Urbana-Champaign.

Kolb, D. G. (1991). Adventure-based professional development: A theory-focused evaluation. Ph.D. dissertation, Cornell University.

Kronour, J. P. (2004). Preservice teaching standards: What skills should first-year teachers possess as they enter the field? Ph.D. dissertation, University of Dayton.

Lacene, K. (1996). Concept mapping wives' adaptation to husbands with brain injuries. M.Ed Thesis, University of Alberta, Canada.

Lassegard, E. (2005). The use of provider and consumer concept maps for the classification and prioritization of mental health services. Ph.D. dissertation, Cornell University.

Lewis, M. F. (2005). Concept mapping school personnel perceptions of adolescent suicide and its prevention. Ph.D. dissertation, State University of New York at Buffalo.

Linton, R. (1985). Conceptualizing feminism: A structured method. Ph.D. dissertation, Cornell University.

Ludwig, S. R. (1996). Abused women's experience with the justice system: Concept mapping. Ph.D. dissertation, University of Alberta, Canada.

Mannes, M. C. (1990). The perceptions of human service workers in planning for the implementation of the family preservation services innovation in Indian child welfare settings. Ph.D. dissertation, Cornell University.

Marquart, J. M. (1988). A pattern matching approach to link program theory and evaluation data: The case of employer-sponsored child care. Ph.D. dissertation, Cornell University.

Martin, M. T. (1999). Students' perceptions of psychologists' characteristics and activities: A concept map and taxonomy. Ph.D. dissertation, Auburn University.

McMurtry, L. J. (1997). James Coleman's theory of social capital as manifest and quantified in a public school setting in southeastern Idaho. Ph.D. dissertation, University of Idaho.

Mensah, D. V. N. (2004). Student campaign against HIV/AIDS in Ghana: A participatory action research (PAR) initiative. Ph.D. dissertation, Cornell University.

Michalski, G. V. (1999). Stakeholder variation in perceptions about training program evaluation. Ph.D. dissertation, University of Ottawa, Canada.

Nelson, E. M. (1999). Internationally-focused managerial behaviors of executives working in large United States multinational corporations. Ph.D. dissertation, University of Illinois at Urbana-Champaign.

Nettina, J. M. (2005). A concept mapping study of the perceived benefits of a therapeutic and recreational camp for grieving children. Ph.D. dissertation, State University of New York at Buffalo.

Phillips, L. J. (1993). Problems faced by adolescents, mothers, and stepfathers while learning to live in a remarried family. Ph.D. dissertation, University of Alberta, Canada.

Plybon, L. E. (2001). Ethnic identity by any other name: A longitudinal analysis of the measurement of ethnic identity in an urban African American early adolescent sample. Ph.D. dissertation, Virginia Commonwealth University.

Purcell, D. L. (1999). Effects on spouses of caring for a partner with dementia. Ph.D. dissertation, University of Alberta, Canada.

Rizzo, M. L. L. (1998). Concept mapping in evaluation practice and theory: A synthesis of current empirical research. Ph.D. dissertation, University of Ottawa, Canada.

Roy, S. M. (1997). Living with chronic pain of rheumatoid arthritis. M.S. Thesis, University of Alberta, Canada.

Rush, S. C. (2004). Teachers' perceptions of working with adolescents with attention-deficit/hyperactivity disorder: A concept-mapping approach. Ph.D. dissertation, University of Alabama.

Sacks, M. L. (1998). Mothers' and fathers' responses to SIDS. Ph.D. dissertation, University of Alberta, Canada.

Schuck, K. (2002). The female managerial experience: A concept map. Ph.D. dissertation, Auburn University.

Sengupta, S. (1995). A similarity-based single study approach to construct and external validity. Ph.D. dissertation, Cornell University.

Setze, R. J. (1994). A nonequivalent dependent variables-pattern matching approach to evaluate program outcomes: The case of a Ph.D. dissertation. PhD, Cornell University.

Stewart, N. F. (2003). Identity, competency, and autonomy of medical social workers in acute care settings. Ph.D. dissertation, University of Texas at Austin.

Stuart, J. M. (2002). Client perceptions of emotional experience in counselling. Ph.D. dissertation, University of Alberta, Canada.

Tittle, M. D. (2001). Assessing university students' epistemological beliefs about foreign language learning. Ph.D. dissertation, University of Illinois at Urbana-Champaign.

Torre, D. A. (1986). Empowerment: Structured conceptualization and instrument development. Ph.D. dissertation, Cornell University.

Weir, D. H. (2001). Rebalancing goals in the National Park Service: Achieving reform in a federal agency. Ph.D. dissertation, Cornell University.

Whitmarsh, B. G. (1998). Athletic pain in competitive swimming. Ph.D. dissertation, University of Alberta, Canada.

Zawallich, A. M. (1997). The experiences of persons with Tourette's syndrome and their family members, as garnered from the Internet. MED thesis, University of Alberta, Canada.

References

Adams, J. L. (1979). *Conceptual blockbusting: A guide to better ideas* (second edition). New York: Norton.

Anderberg, M. R. (1973). *Cluster analysis for applications.* New York: Academic Press.

Anderson, L. A., Gwaltney, M. K., Sundra, D. L., Brownson, R. C., Kane, M., Cross, A. W., et al. (2006). Using concept mapping to develop a logic model for the prevention research centers program. *Preventing Chronic Disease: Public Health Research, Practice and Policy, 3*(1), 1–9.

Baldwin, C. M., Kroesen, K., Trochim, W. M., & Bell, I. R. (2004). Complementary and conventional medicine: A concept map. *BMC Complementary and Alternative Medicine, 4*(2). Retrieved June 29, 2006 from http://www.pubmedcentral.nih.gov/articlerender.fcgi?artid=356920

Batterham, R., Southern, D., Appleby, N., Elsworth, G., Fabris, S., Dunt, D., et al. (2002). Construction of a gp integration model. *Social Science & Medicine, 54*(8), 1225–1241.

Bickman, L. E. (1986). *Using program theory in evaluation.* San Francisco: Jossey-Bass.

Biegel, D. E., Johnsen, J. A., & Shafran, R. (1997). Overcoming barriers faced by African-American families with a family member with mental illness. *Family Relations, 46*(2), 163–178.

Block, J. (1961). The q-sort method in personality assessment and psychiatric research. *American lecture series no. 457.* Springfield, IL: Charles C. Thomas.

Brown, J., & Calder, P. (1999). Concept-mapping the challenges faced by foster parents. *Children and Youth Services Review, 21*(6), 481–495.

Burton, M. L. (1975). Dissimilarity measures for unconstrained sorting data. *Multivariate Behavioral Research, 10*, 409–424.

Caracelli, V. (1989). Structured conceptualization: A framework for interpreting evaluation results. *Evaluation and Program Planning, 12*(1), 45–52.

Caracelli, V. W., & Greene, J. C. (1993). Data analysis strategies for mixed-method evaluation designs. *Educational Evaluation and Policy Analysis, 15*(2), 195–207.

Carpenter, B. D., Van Haitsma, K., Ruckdeschel, K., & Lawton, M. P. (2000). The psychosocial preferences of older adults: A pilot examination of content and structure. *Gerontologist, 40*(3), 335-348.

Cataldo, E. F., Johnson, R. M., Kellstedt, L. A., & Milbrath, L. W. (1970). Card sorting as a technique for survey interviewing. *Public Opinion Quarterly, 34*, 202–215.

Chen, H. T. (1990). *Theory-driven evaluations.* Thousand Oaks, CA: Sage.

Chen, H. T., & Rossi, P. H. (1983). Evaluating with sense: The theory-driven approach. *Evaluation Review, 7*(3), 283–302.

Chen, H. T., & Rossi, P. H. (1987). The theory-driven approach to validity. *Evaluation and Program Planning, 10*, 95–103.

Collaros, P., & Lynn, A. (1969). Effect of perceived expertness upon creativity of members of brainstorming groups. *Journal of Applied Psychology, 53*(2), 159–163.

Concept Systems Incorporated. (2004). *The concept system* (version 3.0). Ithaca, NY: Concept Systems Incorporated.

Concept Systems Incorporated. (2005). The concept system. (Version 4.0). Ithaca, NY: Concept Systems Incorporated. Available at http://www.conceptsystems.com

Cook, T. D., & Campbell, D. T. (1979). *Quasi-experimentation: Design and analysis for field settings.* Boston: Houghton Mifflin.

Cooksy, L. (1989). In the eye of the beholder: Relational and hierarchical structures in conceptualization. *Evaluation and Program Planning, 12*(1), 59–66.

Cordray, D. S. (1986). Quasi-experimental analysis: A mixture of methods and judgment. In W. Trochim (Ed.), *New directions in program evaluation* (pp. 9–28). San Francisco: Jossey-Bass.

Cousins, J. B., & MacDonald, C. J. (1998). Conceptualizing the successful product development project as a basis for evaluating management training in technology-based companies: A participatory concept mapping application. *Evaluation and Program Planning, 21*(3), 333–344.

Coxon, A. P. M. (1999). *Sorting data: Collection and analysis.* Unpublished manuscript.

Daughtry, D., & Kunkel, M. A. (1993). Experience of depression in college students— a concept map. *Journal of Counseling Psychology, 40*(3), 316–323.

Davis, J. (1989). Construct validity in measurement: A pattern matching approach. *Evaluation and Program Planning, 12*(1), 31–36.

Davison, M. L. (1983). *Multidimensional scaling.* New York: John Wiley & Sons.

Delaware Advisory Council on Cancer Incidence and Mortality. (2002). *Turning commitment into action: Recommendations of the Delaware advisory council on cancer incidence and mortality.* Dover: Delaware Department of Health and Social Services, Division of Public Health.

Delbecq, A. L. (1975). *Group techniques for program planning: A guide to nominal group and delphi processes* (Management Applications series). New York: Scott, Foresman.

DeRidder, D., Depla, M., Severens, P., & Malsch, M. (1997). Beliefs on coping with illness: A consumer's perspective. *Social Science & Medicine, 44*(5), 553–559.

Diehl, M., & Wolfgang, S. (1987). Productivity loss in brainstorming groups: Toward the solution of a riddle. *Journal of Personality and Social Psychology, 53* (3), 497–509.

Diehl, M., & Wolfgang, S. (1991). Productivity loss in idea-generating groups: Tracking down the blocking effect. *Journal of Personality and Social Psychology, 61*(3), 392–403.

Donnelly, J. P., Donnelly, K., & Grohman, K. J. (2005). A multi-perspective concept mapping study of problems associated with traumatic brain injury. *Brain Injury, 19*(13), 1077–1085.

Donnelly, J. P., Huff, S. M., Lindsey, M. L., McMahon, K. A., & Schumacher, J. D. (2005). The needs of children with life-limiting conditions: A healthcare-provider-based model. *American Journal of Hospice & Palliative Care, 22*(4), 259–267.

Donnelly, K. Z., Donnelly, J. P., & Grohman, K. J. (2000). Cognitive, emotional, and behavioral problems associated with traumatic brain injury: A concept map of patient, family, and provider perspectives. *Brain and Cognition, 44*(1), 21–25.

Dumont, J. (1989). Validity of multidimensional scaling in the context of structured conceptualization. *Evaluation and Program Planning, 12*(1), 81–86.

Dunn, W. (1981). *Public policy analysis: An introduction.* Englewood Cliffs, NJ: Prentice-Hall.

Einhorn, H. J., & Hogarth, R. M. (1986). Judging probable cause. *Psychological Bulletin, 99*(1), 3–19.

Everitt, B. (1980). *Cluster analysis* (2nd ed.). New York: Halsted Press.

Fillenbaum, S., & Rappaport, A. (1971). *Structures in the subjective lexicon.* New York: Academic Press.

Fowler, F. (2001). *Survey research methods* (3rd ed.). Thousands Oaks, CA: Sage.

Galvin, P. F. (1989). Concept mapping for planning and evaluation of a big brother/ big sister program: Planning and evaluation example. *Evaluation and Program Planning, 12*(1), 53–58.

Greene, J. C., Caracelli, V. J., & Graham, W. F. (1989). Toward a conceptual framework for mixed-method evaluation designs. *Educational Evaluation and Policy Analysis, 11*, 255–274.

Gurowitz, W. D., Trochim, W., & Kramer, H. (1988). A process for planning. *The Journal of the National Association of Student Personnel Administrators, 25*(4), 226–235.

Hair, J. F., Tatham, R. L., Anderson, R. E., & Black, W. C. (1998). *Multivariate data analysis* (5th ed.). New York: Prentice Hall.

Hiltz, S. R., & Turoff, M. (1978). *The network nation: Human communication via computer.* London: Addison-Wesley.

Hurt, L. E., Wiener, R. L., Russell, B. L., & Mannen, R. K. (1999). Gender differences in evaluating social-sexual conduct in the workplace. *Behavioral Sciences & the Law, 17*(4), 413–433.

Jablin, F. (1981). Cultivating imagination: Factors that enhance and inhibit creativity in brainstorming groups. *Human Communication Research, 7* (3), 245–258.

Jackson, K. M., & Trochim, W. M. K. (2002). Concept mapping as an alternative approach for the analysis of open-ended survey responses. *Organizational Research Methods, 5*(4), 307–336.

Johnsen, J. A., Biegel, D. E., & Shafran, R. (2000). Concept mapping in mental health: Uses and adaptations. *Evaluation and Program Planning, 23*(1), 67–75.

Keith, D. (1989). Refining concept maps: Methodological issues and an example. *Evaluation and Program Planning, 12*(1), 75–80.

Kellogg Foundation. (2001). *Logic model development guide: Using logic models to bring together planning, evaluation, and action.* Battle Creek, MI: W. K. Kellogg Foundation.

Krieger, J., Allen, C., Cheadle, A., Ciske, S., Schier, J. K., Senturia, K., et al. (2002). Using community-based participatory research to address social determinants of health: Lessons learned from Seattle partners for healthy communities. *Health Education & Behavior, 29*(3), 361–382.

Krippendorf, K. (2004). *Content analysis: An introduction to its methodology* (2nd ed.). Newbury Park, CA: Sage.

Kruskal, J. B. (1964). Nonmetric multidimensional scaling: A numerical method. *Psychometrika, 29*(2), 115–129.

Kruskal, J. B., & Wish, M. (1978). *Multidimensional scaling.* Beverly Hills, CA: Sage.

Levy, S. (Ed.). (1994). *Louis Guttman on theory and methodology: Selected writings.* Aldershot, England: Dartmouth.

Linstone, H. A., & Turoff, M. (1975). *The delphi method: Techniques and applications.* Reading, MA: Addison-Wesley.

Linton, R. (1989a). Conceptualizing feminism: Clarifying social science concepts. *Evaluation and Program Planning, 12*(1), 25–30.

Linton, R. (1989b). Toward a feminist research method. In A. M. Jagger & S. R. Bordo (Eds.), *Gender/body/knowledge: Feminist reconstructions of being and knowing.* New Brunswick, NJ: Rutgers University Press.

Macaulay, A. C. (1999). Participatory research maximizes community and lay involvement. *British Medical Journal, 319*(7212), 774–778.

Mannes, M. (1989). Using concept mapping for planning the implementation of a social technology. *Evaluation and Program Planning, 12*(1), 67–74.

Mark, M. M. (1986). Validity typologies and the logic and practice of quasi-experimentation. In W. Trochim (Ed.), *Advances in quasi-experimental design and analysis.* San Francisco: Jossey-Bass.

Marquart, J. M. (1989). A pattern matching approach to assess the construct validity of an evaluation instrument. *Evaluation and Program Planning, 12*(1), 37–44.

McKillip, J. (1987). *Needs analysis: Tools for the human services and education.* Newbury Park, CA: Sage.

McLinden, D., & Trochim, W. (1998). Getting to parallel: Assessing the return on expectations of training. *Performance Improvement, 37*(8), 21–25.

McLinden, D., & William, T. (1998). From puzzles to problems: Assessing the impact of education in a business context with concept mapping and pattern matching. *Implementing Evaluation Systems and Processes, the American Society for Training and Development, 18,* 285–304.

Mercier, C., Piat, M., Peladeau, N., & Dagenais, C. (2000). An application of theory-driven evaluation to a drop-in youth center. *Evaluation Review, 24*(1), 73–91.

Michalski, G. V., & Cousins, J. B. (2000). Differences in stakeholder perceptions about training evaluation: A concept mapping/pattern matching investigation. *Evaluation and Program Planning, 23*(2), 211–230.

Moore, C. M. (1987). *Group techniques for idea building.* Beverly Hills, CA: Sage.

Nabitz, U., Severens, P., van den Brink, W., & Jansen, P. (2001). Improving the EFQM model: An empirical study on model development and theory building using concept mapping. *Total Quality Management, 12*(1), 69–81.

National Association of Chronic Disease Directors. (2003). *The healthy aging project: Promoting opportunities for collaboration between the public health and aging services networks.* Atlanta: NACDD.

National Center for Chronic Disease Prevention and Health Promotion. (2003). *Project officer of the future.* Washington, DC: CDC.

Novak, J. D., & Gowin, D. B. (1984). *Learning how to learn.* Cambridge: Cambridge University Press.

Osborn, A. F. (1948). *Your creative power.* New York: Scribner.

Pammer, W., Haney, M., Wood, B. M., Brooks, R. G., Morse, K., Hicks, P., et al. (2001). Use of telehealth technology to extend child protection team services. *Pediatrics, 108*(3), 584–590.

Paulson, B. L., Truscott, D., & Stuart, J. (1999). Clients' perceptions of helpful experiences in counseling. *Journal of Counseling Psychology, 46*(3), 317–324.

Rao, J. K., Alongi, J., Anderson, L. A., Jenkins, L., Stokes, G., & Kane, M. (2005). Development of public health priorities for end-of-life initiatives. *American Journal of Preventive Medicine, 29*(5), 453–460.

Reason, P., & Bradbury, H. (Eds.). (2001). *Handbook of action research: Participative inquiry and practice*. London: Sage.

Rico, G. L. (1983). *Writing the natural way: Using right-brain techniques to release your expressive powers*. Los Angeles: J.P. Tarcher.

Rosas, S. R. (2005). Concept mapping as a technique for program theory development: An illustration using family support programs. *American Journal of Evaluation, 26*(3), 389–401.

Rosenberg, S., & Kim, M. P. (1975). The method of sorting as a data gathering procedure in multivariate research. *Multivariate Behavioral Research, 10,* 489–502.

Rothwell, W. J., & Kazanas, H. C. (1989). *Strategic human resource development*. New Jersey: Prentice Hall.

SAS Institute. (2005). *SAS*. Cary, NC: SAS Institute Inc.

Shadish, W. R., Cook, T. D., & Houts, A. C. (1986). Quasi-experimentation in a critical multiplist mode. In W. Trochim (Ed.), *Advances in quasi-experimental design and analysis*. San Francisco: Jossey-Bass.

Shepard, R. N., Romney, A. K., & Nerlove, S. B. (1972). *Multidimensional scaling: Theory and applications in the behavioral sciences* (Vol. 1). New York: Seminar Press.

Shern, D., Trochim, W., & Lacomb, C. A. (1995). Fidelity of model transfer example: The use of concept mapping for assessing fidelity of model transfer. *Evaluation and Program Planning, 18,* 143–153.

Southern, D. M., Young, D., Dunt, D., Appleby, N. J., & Batterham, R. W. (2002). Integration of primary health care services: Perceptions of Australian general practitioners, non-general practitioner health service providers and consumers at the general practice-primary care interface. *Evaluation and Program Planning, 25*(1), 47–59.

SPSS Inc. (2005). *SPSS*. Chicago: SPSS Inc.

Stefflre, V. J., Reich, P., & McClaran-Stefflre, M. (1971). Some eliciting and computational procedures for descriptive semantics. In P. Kay (Ed.), *Explorations in mathematical anthropology* (pp. 79–116). Cambridge: MIT Press.

Stewart, D. W., & Shamdasani, P. N. (1990). *Focus groups: Theory and practice*. Newbury Park, CA: Sage.

Stokols, D., Fuqua, J., Gress, J., Harvey, R., Phillips, K., Baezconde-Garbanati, L., et al. (2003). Evaluating transdisciplinary science. *Nicotine and Tobacco Research, 5*(Suppl. 1), S21–39.

Stone, P. J., Dunphy, D. C., Smith, M. S., & Ogilvie, D. M. (1966). *The general inquirer: A computer approach to content analysis*. Cambridge: MIT Press.

Trochim, W. (1985). Pattern matching, validity, and conceptualization in program evaluation. *Evaluation Review, 9*(5), 575–604.

Trochim, W. (1989a). Concept mapping for evaluation and planning. *Evaluation and Program Planning, 12*(1), 1–16.

Trochim, W. (1989b). Concept mapping: Soft science or hard art? *Evaluation and Program Planning, 12*(1), 87–110.

Trochim, W. (1989c). An introduction to concept mapping for planning and evaluation. *Evaluation and Program Planning, 12*(1), 1–16.

Trochim, W. (1989d). Outcome pattern matching and program theory. *Evaluation and Program Planning, 12*(1), 355–366.

Trochim, W. (1993). The reliability of concept mapping. Paper presented at the Annual Conference of the American Evaluation Association, Dallas, TX, November 6, 1993.

Trochim, W. (1999). The evaluator as cartographer: Technology for mapping where we're going and where we've been. Paper presented at Conference of the Oregon Program Evaluators Network. Portland, OR. Available at http://www.socialresearchmethods .net/research/OPEN/The%20Evaluator%20as%20Cartographer.pdf

Trochim, W. (2001). *The research methods knowledge base* (2nd ed.). Cincinnati: Atomic Dog Publishing.

Trochim, W. (2004). Concept mapping. In S. Matheson (Ed.), *Encyclopedia of evaluation*. Thousand Oaks, CA: Sage.

Trochim, W., & Cabrera, D. (2005). The complexity of concept mapping. *Emergence: Complexity and Organization, 7*(1), 11–22.

Trochim, W., Cabrera, D., Milstein, B., Gallagher, R., & Leischow, S. (2006). Practical challenges of systems thinking and modeling in public health. *American Journal of Public Health, 96*, 538–546.

Trochim, W., & Cook, J. (1992). Pattern matching in theory-driven evaluation: A field example from psychiatric rehabilitation. In H.-T. Chen & P. H. Rossi (Eds.), *Using Theory to Improve Program and Policy Evaluations* (pp. 49–69). New York: Greenwood Press.

Trochim, W., Cook, J., & Setze, R. (1994). Using concept mapping to develop a conceptual framework of staff's views of a supported employment program for persons with severe mental illness. *Consulting and Clinical Psychology, 62*(4), 766–775.

Trochim, W., & Kane, M. (2005). Concept mapping: An introduction to structured conceptualization in health care. *International Journal for Quality in Health Care, 17*(3), 187–191.

Trochim, W., & Linton, R. (1986). Conceptualization for planning and evaluation. *Evaluation and Program Planning, 9*(4), 289–308.

Trochim, W., Milstein, B., Wood, B., Jackson, S., & Pressler, V. (2004). Setting objectives for community and systems change: An application of concept mapping for planning a statewide health improvement initiative. *Health Promotion Practice, 5*(1), 8–19.

Trochim, W. M. K., Stillman, F. A., Clark, P. I., & Schmitt, C. L. (2003). Development of a model of the tobacco industry's interference with tobacco control programmes. *Tobacco Control, 12*(2), 140–147.

Valacich, J. A. D., & Nunamaker, J. (1992). Group size and anonymity: Effects on computer-mediated idea generation. *Small Group Research, 23*(1), 49–73.

Valentine, K. (1989). Contributions to the theory of care. *Evaluation and Program Planning, 12*(1), 17–24.

van Nieuwenhuizen, C., Schene, A. H., Koeter, M. W. J., & Huxley, P. J. (2001). The Lancashire quality of life profile: Modification and psychometric evaluation. *Social Psychiatry and Psychiatric Epidemiology, 36*(1), 36–44.

VanderWaal, M. A. E., Casparie, A. F., & Lako, C. J. (1996). Quality of care: A comparison of preferences between medical specialists and patients with chronic diseases. *Social Science and Medicine, 42*(5), 643–649.

Veney, J. E., & Kaluzny, A. D. (1984). *Evaluation and decision making for health services programs.* Englewood Cliffs, NJ: Prentice-Hall.

Wasserman, A., & Faust, K. (1994). *Social network analysis: Methods and applications.* Cambridge: Cambridge University Press.

Weller, S. C., & Romney, A. K. (1988). *Systematic data collection.* Newbury Park, CA: Sage Publications.

Wheeler, F., Anderson, L. A., Boddie-Willis, C., Price, P., & Kane, M. (2005). The role of state public health agencies in addressing less prevalent chronic conditions. *Preventing Chronic Disease: Public Health Research, Practice, and Policy, 2*(3), 1–9.

White, K. S., & Farrell, A. D. (2001). Structure of anxiety symptoms in urban children: Competing factor models of the revised children's manifest anxiety scale. *Journal of Consulting and Clinical Psychology, 69*(2), 333–337.

Witkin, B., & Altschuld, J. W. (1995). *Planning and conducting needs assessments.* Thousand Oaks, CA: Sage.

Witkin, B., & Trochim, W. (1997). Toward a synthesis of listening constructs: A concept map analysis of the construct of listening. *International Journal of Listening, 11*, 69–87.

Wrightson, M. (1976). The documentary coding method. In R. Axelrod (Ed.), *The structure of decision: The cognitive maps of political elites.* Princeton, NJ: Princeton University Press.

Index

About the Authors

Mary Kane, M.S., is the president and CEO of Concept Systems Incorporated. The guiding operational force behind CSI's success as a consulting and support company for social and behavioral researchers and managers, Ms. Kane has standardized the CS methodology and process to ensure meaningful, measurable, and useful outcomes for CSI's clients. Consulting experience includes strategic operational planning, leadership coaching and organizational development, product and program development, education and training design, program needs identification, and evaluation planning. She has authored or co-authored several articles on the applications of concept mapping and pattern matching in organizational decision-making and strategic planning, most notably with partners and clients in the areas of public health, community decision making, and evaluation structure development.

Ms. Kane's 25 years in the business of improving public and private organizations has included developing, directing, and managing consulting, facilitation, and training for the wide range of clients in the CSI family. Ms. Kane has developed process and group consulting for federal, state, and county agencies, health and mental health organizations, private corporations, not-for-profit agencies, and school districts; she has facilitated with groups ranging from small boards of directors to organizations represented by thousands of stakeholders.

Ms. Kane co-founded CSI in 1993 after a successful career in the management and growth of community-based cultural and learning organizations.

William M. K. Trochim is a professor in the Department of Policy Analysis and Management and is the Director of Evaluation for Extension and Outreach at Cornell University. He received his PhD from the Department of Psychology at Northwestern University in the area of methodology and evaluation research. His research is broadly in the area of applied social research methodology, with an emphasis on program planning and evaluation methods. Among experimentalists, he is known for his work in quasi-experimental alternatives to randomized experimental designs, especially the regression discontinuity and regression point displacement designs. In terms of research theory, he has extended the theory of validity through his articulation and investigation of the idea of pattern matching. In multivariate and applied contexts, he is recognized for the development of a multivariate form of structured conceptual mapping, a general method for mapping the ideas of a group of people on any topic of interest that integrates traditional group processes (e.g., brainstorming, Delphi, focus groups, nominal group technique) with multivariate statistical methods (e.g., multidimensional scaling, hierarchical cluster analysis).

Dr. Trochim has written or edited several books and monographs, is the author of several widely used introductory research methods texts, and has written articles that have appeared in *American Journal of Evaluation, New Directions for Program Evaluation, Evaluation and Program Planning, Evaluation Review, American Journal of Public Health, Journal of Clinical Epidemiology, Consulting and Clinical Psychology, Controlled Clinical Trials, Performance Improvement,* and *Medical Decision Making,* among others. He is the developer of the Concept System software and methodology and co-founder of Concept Systems Incorporated, a company that provides the software, training, and consulting services to support the method. He has also been an active member of the American Evaluation Association, serving multiple terms on its board.

Sort by valid/reliable = forensic
Loss Pre/Post evidence/concept
Fauning Concepts / elements/ factors / variables
Capacity Measures /processes
that are summative of
Past performance of
the N=1 & predictive
of future performance
+ Interventions that
may differences in future
predictive outcomes